AMERICA'S FAVORITE BRAND NAME

BEST-LOVED CHICKEN RECIPES

Wings & Things, 2

Super Soups, Stews & Salads, 20

Down-Home Favorites, 34

International Flavors, 52

Hot off the Grill, 68

BEST-LOVED
Chicken Recipes

WINGS & THINGS

Hot & Spicy Buffalo Chicken Wings

Prep Time: 5 minutes
Cook Time: 35 minutes

**1 can (15 ounces) DEL MONTE®
   Original Sloppy Joe Sauce**
**¼ cup thick and chunky salsa,
   medium**
**1 tablespoon red wine vinegar or
   cider vinegar**
**20 chicken wings
   (about 4 pounds)**

1. Preheat oven to 400°F.

2. Combine sloppy joe sauce, salsa and vinegar in small bowl. Remove ¼ cup sauce mixture to serve with cooked chicken wings; cover and refrigerate. Set aside remaining sauce mixture.

3. Arrange wings in single layer in large, shallow baking pan; brush wings with sauce mixture.

4. Bake chicken, uncovered, on middle rack in oven 35 minutes or until chicken is no longer pink in center, turning and brushing with remaining sauce mixture after 15 minutes. Serve with reserved ¼ cup sauce. Garnish, if desired.   *Makes 4 servings*

Taco Chicken Nachos

2 small boneless skinless chicken breasts (about 8 ounces)
1 tablespoon plus 1½ teaspoons taco seasoning mix
1 teaspoon olive oil
¾ cup nonfat sour cream
1 can (4 ounces) chopped mild green chilies, drained
¼ cup minced red onion
1 bag (8 ounces) baked nonfat tortilla chips
1 cup (4 ounces) shredded reduced-fat Cheddar or Monterey Jack cheese
½ cup chopped tomato
¼ cup pitted ripe olive slices (optional)
2 tablespoons chopped fresh cilantro (optional)

1. Bring 2 cups water to boil in small saucepan. Add chicken. Reduce heat to low; cover. Simmer 10 minutes or until chicken is no longer pink in center. Remove from saucepan; cool. Chop chicken.

2. Combine taco seasoning mix and oil in small bowl; mix until smooth paste forms. Stir in sour cream. Add chicken, green chilies and onion; mix well.

3. Preheat broiler. Arrange tortilla chips on baking sheet; cover chips with chicken mixture and cheese. Broil 4 inches from heat 2 to 3 minutes or until chicken mixture is hot and cheese is melted. Sprinkle evenly with tomato, olives, and cilantro, if desired.
Makes 12 servings

Buffalo Bar-B-Q Nuggets

Prep Time: 10 minutes
Marinate Time: 20 minutes
Cook Time: 10 minutes

½ cup Frank's® RedHot® Sauce
⅓ cup butter, melted
1½ pounds boneless skinless chicken thighs or breasts
Lettuce leaves
Blue cheese salad dressing (optional)

1. Combine **RedHot** Sauce and butter in small bowl; mix well. Reserve ⅓ cup sauce mixture. Pour remaining sauce over chicken. Cover; refrigerate 20 minutes. Prepare grill.

2. Discard remaining chicken marinade. Place chicken on oiled grid. Grill, over medium coals, about 10 minutes or until no longer pink in center. Heat reserved sauce. Cut chicken into bite-size pieces; toss chicken pieces in warmed sauce.

3. Arrange chicken on lettuce-lined serving platter. Serve with blue cheese dressing, if desired.
Makes 6 to 8 servings

Taco Chicken Nachos

Party Chicken Tarts

2 tablespoons butter or
   margarine
1 cup chopped fresh mushrooms
¼ cup finely chopped celery
¼ cup finely chopped onion
2 tablespoons all-purpose flour
1½ cups chopped cooked chicken
6 tablespoons sour cream
½ teaspoon garlic salt
1 package (10 ounces) flaky
   refrigerator biscuits (10 to
   12 count)
   Vegetable cooking spray
1 tablespoon butter or
   margarine, melted
   Grated Parmesan cheese

Melt 2 tablespoons butter in large skillet until hot. Add mushrooms, celery and onion; cook and stir 4 to 5 minutes. Sprinkle with flour; stir in chicken and sour cream. Cook until thoroughly heated. Stir in garlic salt; set aside. Cut each biscuit into quarters; press each piece into miniature muffin tins coated with cooking spray to form tart shell. Brush each piece with melted butter. Bake at 400°F 6 minutes. Remove from oven; reduce oven temperature to 350°F. Fill each tart with 1 teaspoon chicken mixture; sprinkle with cheese. Bake 14 to 15 minutes more. Serve immediately.

Makes 40 to 48 appetizers

Note: For ease in serving at party time, prepare filling ahead and cook tarts 5 minutes. Fill and bake just before serving for best flavor.

Favorite recipe from **National Broiler Council**

Sticky Wings

24 chicken wings (about
   4 pounds)
¾ cup WISH-BONE® Italian
   Dressing*
1 cup apricot or peach
   preserves
1 tablespoon hot pepper sauce
   (optional)**

Also terrific with WISH-BONE® Robusto Italian or Just 2 Good Dressing.

**Use more or less to taste desired.*

Cut tips off chicken wings (save tips for soup). Cut chicken wings in half at joint.

For marinade, blend Italian dressing, preserves and hot pepper sauce. In large, shallow nonaluminum baking dish or plastic bag, pour ½ of the marinade over chicken wings; toss to coat. Cover, or close bag, and marinate in refrigerator, turning occasionally, 3 to 24 hours. Refrigerate remaining marinade.

Remove wings, discarding marinade. Grill or broil wings, turning once and brushing frequently with refrigerated marinade, until wings are done.

Makes 48 appetizers

Ranch Buffalo Wings

½ cup butter or margarine, melted
¼ cup hot pepper sauce
3 tablespoons vinegar
24 chicken wing drumettes
1 package (1 ounce) HIDDEN VALLEY® Milk Recipe Original Ranch® Salad Dressing Mix
½ teaspoon paprika
1 cup prepared HIDDEN VALLEY® Original Ranch® Salad Dressing
Celery sticks

Preheat oven to 350°F. In small bowl, whisk together butter, pepper sauce and vinegar. Dip drumettes into butter mixture; arrange in single layer in large baking pan. Sprinkle with 1 package salad dressing mix. Bake 30 to 40 minutes or until chicken is browned and juices run clear. Sprinkle with paprika. Serve with prepared salad dressing and celery sticks.
Makes 6 to 8 servings

Red Hot Pepper Wings

28 chicken wing drumettes (2¼ to 3 pounds)
2 tablespoons olive oil
Salt and black pepper
¼ to ½ cup hot pepper sauce
2 tablespoons melted butter
1 teaspoon sugar

Brush chicken with oil; sprinkle with salt and pepper. Grill chicken on covered grill over medium KINGSFORD® Briquets

about 20 minutes until juices run clear, turning every 5 minutes. Combine butter, sugar and pepper sauce in large bowl; add chicken and toss to coat. Serve hot or cold.
Makes 7 servings

Curried Buffalo Wings

15 chicken wings (about 3 pounds)
¼ cup I CAN'T BELIEVE IT'S NOT BUTTER!® Spread
1 tablespoon mild or hot curry powder
2 teaspoons chopped garlic
1 teaspoon salt

Preheat oven to 450°F.

Cut tips off chicken wings (save tips for soup). Cut chicken wings in half at joint; set aside.

In 12-inch skillet, melt I Can't Believe It's Not Butter! Spread over medium heat and cook curry, garlic and salt, stirring frequently, 30 seconds or until curry darkens slightly; set aside.

In bottom of broiler pan, without rack, pour curry sauce over chicken wings and toss to coat. Bake 35 minutes or until chicken wings are golden brown and fully cooked.
Makes 30 appetizers

7

Coconut Chicken Tenders with Spicy Mango Salsa

1 firm ripe mango, peeled, seeded and chopped
½ cup chopped red bell pepper
3 tablespoons chopped green onion
2 tablespoons chopped fresh cilantro
Salt
Dash ground red pepper
1½ cups flaked coconut
1 egg
1 tablespoon vegetable oil
¾ pound chicken tenders

Combine mango, bell pepper, onion and cilantro in small bowl. Season to taste with salt and ground red pepper.

Transfer half of salsa to food processor; process until finely chopped (almost puréed). Combine with remaining salsa.

Preheat oven to 400°F. Spread coconut on large baking sheet. Bake 5 to 6 minutes or until lightly browned, stirring every 2 minutes. Transfer coconut to food processor; process until finely chopped but not pasty.

Beat egg with oil, salt and ground red pepper in small bowl. Add chicken tenders; toss to coat. Roll tenders in coconut; arrange on foil-lined baking sheet. Bake 18 to 20 minutes or until no longer pink in center. Serve with spicy mango salsa.

Makes 5 to 6 servings

Buffalo Chicken Wings

24 chicken wings
1 teaspoon salt
¼ teaspoon ground black pepper
4 cups vegetable oil for frying
¼ cup butter or margarine
¼ cup hot pepper sauce
1 teaspoon white wine vinegar
Celery sticks
1 bottle (8 ounces) blue cheese dressing

Cut tips off wings at first joint; discard tips. Cut remaining wings into two parts at the joint; sprinkle with salt and pepper. Heat oil in deep fryer or heavy saucepan to 375°F. Add half the wings; fry about 10 minutes or until golden brown and crisp, stirring occasionally. Remove with slotted spoon; drain on paper towels. Repeat with remaining wings.

Melt butter in small saucepan over medium heat; stir in pepper sauce and vinegar. Cook until thoroughly heated. Place wings on large platter. Pour sauce over wings. Serve warm with celery and dressing for dipping.

Makes 24 appetizers

Favorite recipe from **National Chicken Council**

Buffalo Chicken Wings

Garlicky Gilroy Chicken Wings

2 heads fresh garlic, separated into cloves and peeled
1 cup olive oil plus additional for greasing
1 teaspoon hot pepper sauce
1 cup grated Parmesan cheese
1 cup Italian-style bread crumbs
1 teaspoon black pepper
2 pounds chicken wings

Place garlic, 1 cup oil and hot pepper sauce in food processor; cover and process until smooth. Pour garlic mixture into bowl. Combine cheese, bread crumbs and pepper in shallow dish. Dip wings, one at a time, into garlic mixture, then roll in crumb mixture, coating evenly.

Grease 13×9-inch nonstick baking pan; arrange wings in single layer in pan. Drizzle remaining garlic mixture over wings; sprinkle with remaining crumb mixture. Bake 45 to 60 minutes or until wings are brown and crisp.

Makes about 6 servings

Sunshine Chicken Drumsticks

½ cup A.1.® Steak Sauce
¼ cup ketchup
¼ cup apricot preserves
12 chicken drumsticks (about 2½ pounds)

Blend steak sauce, ketchup and preserves in small bowl with wire whisk until smooth. Brush chicken with sauce.

Grill chicken over medium heat for 20 minutes or until no longer pink, turning and brushing with remaining sauce. (Do not baste during last 5 minutes of grilling.) Serve hot.

Makes 12 appetizers

Spicy Wings

16 chicken wings
½ cup olive or vegetable oil
¼ cup balsamic vinegar
¼ cup honey
2 tablespoons brown sugar
2 tablespoons cane syrup or dark corn syrup
1 tablespoon TABASCO® brand Pepper Sauce
1 teaspoon soy sauce
½ teaspoon dried thyme leaves
¼ teaspoon ground nutmeg
¼ teaspoon Worcestershire sauce

Cut off and discard bony wing tips. Cut remaining wings in half. Combine remaining ingredients in large bowl until well blended; add wings. Cover and marinate in refrigerator 1 hour.

Prepare grill. Place wings on grid. Grill 15 to 20 minutes over medium coals, turning frequently.

Makes 32 appetizers

Sunshine Chicken Drumsticks

Pesto Chicken Brushetta

2 tablespoons olive oil, divided
1 teaspoon coarsely chopped
   garlic, divided
8 diagonal slices (¼ inch thick)
   sourdough bread, divided
½ cup (2 ounces) grated
   BELGIOIOSO® Asiago Cheese,
   divided
2 tablespoons prepared pesto
¼ teaspoon pepper
4 boneless skinless chicken
   breast halves
12 slices (¼ inch thick)
   BELGIOIOSO® Fresh
   Mozzarella Cheese
   (8 ounces)
2 tomatoes, each cut into
   4 slices

In 10-inch skillet, heat 1 tablespoon olive oil and ½ teaspoon garlic. Add 4 slices bread. Cook over medium-high heat, turning once, 5 to 7 minutes or until toasted. Remove from pan. Add remaining 1 tablespoon oil and ½ teaspoon garlic; repeat with remaining bread slices. Sprinkle ¼ cup BelGioioso Asiago Cheese on bread. In same skillet, combine pesto and pepper. Add chicken, coating with pesto. Cook over medium-high heat, turning once, 8 to 10 minutes or until chicken is brown. Place 3 slices BelGioioso Fresh Mozzarella Cheese on each bread slice; top with tomato slice. Slice chicken pieces in half horizontally; place on tomato. Sprinkle with remaining BelGioioso Asiago Cheese. *Makes 4 servings*

Almond Chicken Cups

Prep and Cook Time: 30 minutes

1 tablespoon vegetable oil
½ cup chopped red bell pepper
½ cup chopped onion
2 cups chopped cooked chicken
⅔ cup prepared sweet-sour sauce
½ cup chopped almonds
2 tablespoons soy sauce
6 (6- or 7-inch) flour tortillas

1. Preheat oven to 400°F. Heat oil in small skillet over medium heat until hot. Add bell pepper and onion. Cook and stir 3 minutes or until crisp-tender.

2. Combine vegetable mixture, chicken, sweet-sour sauce, almonds and soy sauce in medium bowl; mix until well blended.

3. Cut each tortilla in half. Place each half in 2¾-inch muffin cup. Fill each with about ¼ cup chicken mixture.

4. Bake 8 to 10 minutes or until tortilla edges are crisp and filling is hot. Remove muffin pan to cooling rack. Let stand 5 minutes before serving.
Makes 12 chicken cups

Almond Chicken Kabobs

- ⅓ cup A.1.® BOLD & SPICY Steak Sauce
- 1 tablespoon GREY POUPON® Dijon Mustard
- 1 tablespoon honey
- 1 tablespoon vegetable oil
- 1 tablespoon lemon juice
- 1 clove garlic, crushed
- 4 boneless skinless chicken breast halves (about 1 pound)
- ¼ cup toasted slivered almonds, finely chopped

Blend steak sauce, mustard, honey, oil, lemon juice and garlic; set aside.

Cut each chicken breast half into 8 cubes. Combine chicken cubes and ½ cup steak sauce mixture in nonmetal bowl. Cover; refrigerate 1 hour, turning occasionally.

Soak 16 (10-inch) wooden skewers in water for at least 30 minutes. Thread 2 chicken cubes onto each skewer. Grill kabobs over medium heat for 6 to 8 minutes or until done, turning and brushing with remaining sauce. Remove from grill; quickly roll kabobs in almonds. Serve immediately.

Makes 16 appetizers

Hot & Cool Teriyaki Wings

- 4 pounds chicken wings (about 20 wings)
- ¾ cup KIKKOMAN® Teriyaki Marinade & Sauce
- 2 teaspoons crushed red pepper
- ¾ teaspoon hot pepper sauce Cool Teriyaki Dipping Sauce (recipe follows)

Discard chicken wing tips (or save for stock); place wings in large plastic food storage bag. Combine teriyaki sauce, crushed red pepper and pepper sauce; pour over wings. Press air out of bag; close top securely. Turn bag over several times to coat all pieces well. Refrigerate 8 hours or overnight. Remove wings; place on grill 4 to 5 inches from hot coals. Cook 20 to 25 minutes, or until tender, turning over frequently. (Or, place on rack of broiler pan. Broil 4 to 5 inches from heat 20 to 25 minutes, or until tender, turning over frequently.) Meanwhile, prepare Cool Teriyaki Dipping Sauce. Serve with wings.

Makes 4 servings

Cool Teriyaki Dipping Sauce:
Combine ¾ cup sour cream, ⅓ cup mayonnaise, 1 tablespoon *each* minced green onions, minced fresh parsley and KIKKOMAN® Teriyaki Sauce. Refrigerate until ready to serve.

Almond Chicken Kabobs

Party Chicken Sandwiches

Prep: 10 minutes
Broil: 5 minutes

1½ **cups finely chopped cooked chicken**
 1 **cup MIRACLE WHIP® or MIRACLE WHIP LIGHT Dressing**
 1 **can (4 ounces) chopped green chilies, drained**
 ¾ **cup (3 ounces) KRAFT® Shredded Sharp Cheddar Cheese**
 ¼ **cup finely chopped onion**
36 **party rye or pumpernickel bread slices**

HEAT broiler.

MIX chicken, dressing, chilies, cheese and onion. Spread evenly onto bread slices.

BROIL 5 minutes or until lightly browned. Serve hot.   *Makes 3 dozen*

Make-Ahead: Prepare chicken mixture as directed; cover. Refrigerate. When ready to serve, spread bread with chicken mixture. Broil as directed.

Sesame Chicken Nuggets

2 **tablespoons sesame seeds**
1 **tablespoon Worcestershire sauce**
1 **tablespoon water**
1 **teaspoon granulated sugar**
1 **teaspoon chili powder**
¼ **teaspoon garlic powder**
1 **pound boneless chicken breasts, skinned and cut into 1-inch cubes**
 Barbecue Sauce (recipe follows)

In small bowl, combine all ingredients except chicken and Barbecue Sauce; mix well. Add chicken and coat evenly. Spread on broiling pan. Broil 10 minutes or until lightly browned, turning once. Serve with Barbecue Sauce or stuff into pita pockets with lettuce and sliced tomato.

Note: This recipe can be doubled for an easy dinner dish. Serve any leftover chicken nuggets in pita pocket sandwiches.

BARBECUE SAUCE:

1 **can (8 ounces) tomato sauce**
1 **teaspoon granulated sugar**
1 **teaspoon red wine vinegar**
½ **teaspoon Worcestershire sauce**
½ **teaspoon chili powder**
¼ **teaspoon garlic powder**

In medium saucepan, combine all ingredients; simmer 15 minutes, stirring occasionally. Use as a dipping sauce for chicken nuggets.   *Makes 1 cup*

Favorite recipe from **The Sugar Association, Inc.**

Tortilla Crunch Chicken Fingers

1 envelope LIPTON® RECIPE SECRETS® Savory Herb with Garlic Soup Mix
1 cup finely crushed plain tortilla chips or cornflakes (about 3 ounces)
1½ pounds boneless, skinless chicken breasts, cut into strips
1 egg
2 tablespoons water
2 tablespoons margarine or butter, melted

Preheat oven to 400°F.

In medium bowl, combine savory herb with garlic soup mix and tortilla chips. In large plastic bag or bowl, combine chicken and egg beaten with water until evenly coated. Remove chicken and dip in tortilla mixture until evenly coated; discard bag. On 15½×10½×1-inch jelly-roll pan sprayed with nonstick cooking spray, arrange chicken; drizzle with margarine. Bake, uncovered, 12 minutes or until chicken is done.

Makes about 24 chicken fingers

Tip: Serve chicken with your favorite fresh or prepared salsa.

Sweet & Spicy Drumettes

1¾ cups (16-ounce jar) ORTEGA® Green Chile Picante Sauce, medium, divided
⅓ cup honey
¼ cup soy sauce
¼ cup Dijon mustard
2 pounds (about 20) chicken wing drumettes

COMBINE 1 cup picante sauce, honey, soy sauce and mustard in large bowl or in large resealable plastic food-storage bag.

ADD drumettes; toss to coat well. Marinate in refrigerator for at least 2 hours.

PLACE chicken on greased or foil-lined baking pan. Bake in preheated 375°F oven for 30 to 35 minutes or until no longer pink near bone. Serve with remaining ¾ cup picante sauce for dipping. *Makes 20 appetizers*

Ginger Wings with Peach Dipping Sauce

Peach Dipping Sauce (recipe follows)
2 pounds chicken wings
¼ cup soy sauce
2 cloves garlic, minced
1 teaspoon ground ginger
¼ teaspoon white pepper

1. Preheat oven to 400°F. Line 15×10×1-inch jelly-roll pan with foil; set aside. Prepare Peach Dipping Sauce; set aside.

2. Cut off and discard wing tips from chicken. Cut each wing in half at joint. Combine soy sauce, garlic, ginger and pepper in large bowl. Add chicken and stir until well coated. Place chicken in single layer in prepared pan. Bake 40 to 50 minutes or until browned, turning over halfway through cooking time. Serve hot with Peach Dipping Sauce.

Makes 6 appetizer servings

Peach Dipping Sauce

½ cup peach preserves
2 tablespoons light corn syrup
1 teaspoon white vinegar
¼ teaspoon ground ginger
¾ teaspoon soy sauce

Combine preserves, corn syrup, vinegar and ginger in small saucepan. Cook and stir over medium-high heat until mixture simmers. Remove from heat; add soy sauce. Let cool.

Makes ½ cup

Gorgonzola Buffalo Wings

Dressing
¼ cup mayonnaise
3 tablespoons sour cream
1½ tablespoons white wine vinegar
¼ teaspoon sugar
⅓ cup (1½ ounces) BELGIOIOSO® Gorgonzola

Chicken
2 pounds chicken wings
3 tablespoons hot pepper sauce
1 tablespoon vegetable oil
1 clove garlic, minced

For dressing
Combine mayonnaise, sour cream, vinegar and sugar in small bowl. Stir in BelGioioso Gorgonzola; cover and refrigerate until serving.

For chicken
Place chicken in large resealable plastic food storage bag. Combine pepper sauce, oil and garlic in separate small bowl; pour over chicken. Seal bag tightly; turn to coat. Marinate in refrigerator at least 1 hour or, for hotter flavor, up to 24 hours, turning occasionally.

Prepare grill. Drain chicken, discarding marinade. Place chicken on grill. Grill on covered grill over medium-hot coals or until chicken is no longer pink, turning 3 to 4 times. Serve with dressing.

Makes 4 servings

Ginger Wings with Peach Dipping Sauce

18

BEST-LOVED
Chicken Recipes

SUPER SOUPS, STEWS & SALADS

Country Chicken Stew

Prep Time: 5 minutes
Cook Time: 20 minutes

2 tablespoons butter or margarine
1 pound boneless skinless chicken breasts, cut into 1-inch cubes
½ pound small red potatoes, cut into ½-inch cubes
2 tablespoons cooking sherry
2 jars (12 ounces each) golden chicken gravy
1 bag (16 ounces) BIRDS EYE® frozen Farm Fresh Mixtures Broccoli, Green Beans, Pearl Onions and Red Peppers
½ cup water

• Melt butter in large saucepan over high heat. Add chicken and potatoes; cook about 8 minutes or until browned, stirring frequently.

• Add sherry; cook until evaporated. Add gravy, vegetables and water.

• Bring to boil; reduce heat to medium-low. Cover and cook 5 minutes. *Makes 4 to 6 servings*

Southwestern Chicken Soup

Prep Time: 10 minutes
Cook Time: 22 minutes

½ **teaspoon salt**
¼ **teaspoon garlic powder**
¼ **teaspoon black pepper**
1 **pound boneless skinless chicken breast halves**
1 **tablespoon olive oil**
1 **medium onion, halved and sliced**
1 **small hot chili pepper,* seeded and chopped (optional)**
4 **cans (about 14 ounces each) fat-free reduced-sodium chicken broth**
2 **cups peeled and diced potatoes**
2 **small zucchini, sliced**
1½ **cups frozen corn**
1 **cup diced tomato**
2 **tablespoons lime or lemon juice**
1 **tablespoon chopped fresh cilantro**

*Hot chili peppers can sting and irritate the skin; wear rubber gloves when handling peppers and do not touch eyes. Wash hands after handling.

1. Combine salt, garlic powder and black pepper in small bowl; sprinkle evenly over chicken.

2. Heat oil in Dutch oven over medium-high heat. Add chicken; cook, without stirring, 2 minutes or until golden. Turn chicken and cook 2 minutes more. Add onion and chili pepper, if desired; cook 2 minutes longer, adding a little chicken broth if needed, to prevent burning.

3. Add chicken broth; bring to a boil. Stir in potatoes. Reduce heat to low; cook 5 minutes. Add zucchini, corn and tomato; cook 10 minutes longer or until vegetables are tender. Just before serving, stir in lime juice and cilantro.   *Makes 6 servings*

Salsa Corn Soup with Chicken

3 **quarts chicken broth**
2 **pounds boneless skinless chicken breasts, cooked and diced**
2 **packages (10 ounces each) frozen whole kernel corn, thawed**
4 **jars (11 ounces each) NEWMAN'S OWN® All Natural Salsa**
4 **large carrots, diced**

Bring chicken broth to a boil in Dutch oven. Add chicken, corn, Newman's Own® Salsa and carrots. Bring to a boil. Reduce heat and simmer until carrots are tender.

Makes 8 servings

Southwestern Chicken Soup

Tomato Chicken Gumbo

Prep and Cook Time: *1 hour*

6 chicken thighs
½ pound hot sausage links or Polish sausage, sliced
3 cups water
1 can (14 ounces) chicken broth
½ cup uncooked long-grain white rice
1 can (26 ounces) DEL MONTE® Traditional or Chunky Garlic and Herb Spaghetti Sauce
1 can (11 ounces) DEL MONTE SUMMER CRISP™ Whole Kernel Golden Sweet Corn, drained
1 medium green bell pepper, diced

1. Preheat oven to 400°F. In large shallow baking pan, place chicken and sausage. Bake 35 minutes or until chicken is no longer pink in center. Cool slightly.

2. Remove skin from chicken; cut meat into cubes. Cut sausage into slices ½ inch thick.

3. Bring water and broth to boil in 6-quart pot. Add chicken, sausage and rice. Cover; cook over medium heat 15 minutes.

4. Stir in remaining ingredients; bring to boil. Cover; cook 5 minutes or until rice is tender.   *Makes 4 servings*

Tip: Add additional water or broth for a thinner gumbo. For spicier gumbo, serve with hot red pepper sauce.

Tomato Chicken Gumbo

Pantry Soup

½ cup dry pasta (rotini or rotelle), cooked and drained
2 teaspoons olive oil
8 ounces boneless skinless chicken, cubed
2 cans (14.5 ounces each) CONTADINA® Diced Tomatoes with Italian Herbs, undrained
¾ cup chicken broth
¾ cup water
1 cup garbanzo beans, undrained
1 cup kidney beans, undrained
1 package (16 ounces) frozen mixed vegetables
2 teaspoons lemon juice

1. Heat oil in 5-quart saucepan with lid; sauté chicken about 3 to 4 minutes or until cooked, stirring occasionally.

2. Mix in tomatoes, broth, water, garbanzo and kidney beans; cover and bring to a boil. Add mixed vegetables and pasta; bring to boil.

3. Reduce heat; cover and simmer 3 minutes or until vegetables are tender. Stir in lemon juice; serve with condiments, if desired.

Makes 6 to 8 servings

Optional Condiments: Grated Parmesan cheese, chopped fresh basil or parsley, or croutons.

Chicken Curry Soup

6 ounces boneless skinless chicken breast, cut into ½-inch pieces
3½ teaspoons curry powder, divided
1 teaspoon olive oil
¾ cup chopped apple
½ cup sliced carrot
⅓ cup sliced celery
¼ teaspoon ground cloves
2 cans (about 14 ounces each) fat-free reduced-sodium chicken broth
½ cup orange juice
4 ounces uncooked radiatore pasta
Plain nonfat yogurt (optional)

1. Coat chicken with 3 teaspoons curry powder. Heat oil in large saucepan over medium heat until hot. Add chicken; cook and stir 3 minutes or until no longer pink in center. Remove from pan; set aside.

2. Add apple, carrot, celery, remaining ½ teaspoon curry powder and cloves to same pan; cook, stirring occasionally, 5 minutes. Add chicken broth and orange juice; bring to a boil over high heat.

3. Reduce heat to medium-low. Add pasta; cover. Cook, stirring occasionally, 8 to 10 minutes or until pasta is tender; add chicken. Remove from heat. Ladle into soup tureen or individual bowls. Top each serving with a dollop of yogurt, if desired.

Makes 4 (¾-cup) servings

25

Cobb Salad with Tarragon Dressing

Prep Time: 45 minutes

TARRAGON DRESSING
- 1 cup plain yogurt
- ½ cup reduced-fat mayonnaise
- ½ cup chopped fresh parsley
- 4 tablespoons chopped fresh tarragon *or* 1 tablespoon dried tarragon leaves
- ¼ cup milk
- 3 tablespoons *Frank's® RedHot®* Sauce
- 2 tablespoons lime juice
- 2 teaspoons honey

SALAD
- 8 cups thinly sliced Romaine lettuce
- 2 cups (10 ounces) chopped cooked chicken
- 6 slices crisply cooked bacon, crumbled
- 3 hard-cooked eggs, cut into wedges
- 4 plum tomatoes, diced
- 1 can (8¼ ounces) sliced beets, drained and cut into strips
- 1 small ripe avocado, diced
- 1 small red onion, diced
- 1½ cups diced seeded cucumber
- ½ cup (2 ounces) crumbled Gorgonzola cheese

1. Combine dressing ingredients in medium bowl; mix until well blended.

2. Arrange lettuce on serving platter or in 8 individual salad bowls. Arrange chicken, bacon, eggs, tomatoes, beets, avocado, onion, cucumber and Gorgonzola in mounds or rows over lettuce. Serve with Tarragon Dressing.

Makes 8 servings (2 cups dressing)

BLT Chicken Salad for Two

- 2 boneless skinless chicken breast halves
- ¼ cup mayonnaise or salad dressing
- ½ teaspoon black pepper
- 4 large leaf lettuce leaves
- 1 large tomato, seeded and diced
- 3 slices crisp-cooked bacon, crumbled
- 1 hard-cooked egg, sliced
  Additional mayonnaise or salad dressing (optional)

1. Brush chicken with mayonnaise; sprinkle with pepper. Grill over hot coals 5 to 7 minutes per side or until no longer pink in center. Cool slightly; cut into thin strips.

2. Arrange lettuce leaves on serving plates. Top with chicken, tomato, bacon and egg. Spoon additional mayonnaise over top, if desired.

Makes 2 servings

Tropical Chicken Salad

Tropical Salad Dressing (recipe follows)
3 cups cubed cooked chicken
¾ cup coarsely chopped celery
¾ cup seedless red or green grape halves
¾ cup coarsely chopped macadamia nuts or toasted almonds
Lettuce leaves
Strawberries and kiwifruit for garnish
Toasted flaked coconut for garnish*

To toast coconut, spread evenly on cookie sheet. Toast in preheated 350°F oven 7 minutes. Stir and toast 1 to 2 minutes more or until light golden brown.

Prepare Tropical Salad Dressing. Combine chicken, celery, grapes and nuts in large bowl; stir in 1 cup dressing. Cover; refrigerate 1 hour. Mound chicken salad on lettuce-lined platter or individual plates. Garnish with strawberries, kiwifruit and coconut. Serve with remaining dressing. *Makes 4 servings*

Tropical Salad Dressing: Place ½ cup cream of coconut, ⅓ cup red wine vinegar, 1 teaspoon dry mustard, 1 teaspoon salt and 1 clove garlic, peeled, in blender or food processor container. With processor on, slowly add 1 cup vegetable oil in thin stream, processing until smooth.

Black Bean and Mango Chicken Salad

Prep: *10 minutes plus refrigerating*

1 can (16 ounces) black beans, drained, rinsed
1 package (10 ounces) frozen corn, thawed
1 cup chopped ripe mango
½ pound boneless skinless chicken breasts, grilled, cut up
½ cup chopped red pepper
⅓ cup chopped fresh cilantro
⅓ cup chopped red onion
¼ cup lime juice
1 envelope GOOD SEASONS® Italian Salad Dressing Mix

TOSS all ingredients in large bowl. Refrigerate.

SERVE with baked tortilla chips, if desired. *Makes 4 servings*

Black Bean and Mango Chicken Salad

Chili-Crusted Grilled Chicken Caesar Salad

1 to 2 lemons
1 tablespoon minced garlic, divided
1½ teaspoons dried oregano leaves, crushed, divided
1 teaspoon chili powder
1 pound boneless skinless chicken breasts
1 tablespoon olive oil
2 anchovy fillets, minced
1 large head romaine lettuce, cut into 1-inch strips
¼ cup grated Parmesan cheese
4 whole wheat rolls

1. Grate lemon peel; measure 1 to 2 teaspoons. Juice lemon; measure ¼ cup. Combine lemon peel and 1 tablespoon juice in small bowl. Set ¼ teaspoon garlic aside. Add remaining garlic, 1 teaspoon oregano and chili powder to lemon peel mixture; stir to combine. Rub chicken with lemon peel mixture.

2. Combine remaining 3 tablespoons lemon juice, ¼ teaspoon garlic, remaining ½ teaspoon oregano, oil and anchovies in large bowl. Add lettuce; toss to coat. Sprinkle with cheese; toss.

3. Spray cold grid with nonstick cooking spray. Prepare grill for direct grilling. Place chicken on grid 3 to 4 inches above medium-hot coals. Grill chicken 5 to 6 minutes. Turn chicken; grill 3 to 4 minutes or until chicken is no longer pink in center.

4. Arrange salad on 4 large plates. Slice chicken; fan on each salad. Serve with whole wheat rolls.

Makes 4 servings

Blue Cheese Chicken Salad

Prep Time: 10 minutes
Cook Time: 10 minutes

1 can (14½ ounces) DEL MONTE® Diced Tomatoes with Garlic & Onion
½ pound boneless, skinned chicken breasts, cut into strips
½ teaspoon dried tarragon
6 cups torn assorted lettuces
½ medium red onion, thinly sliced
½ medium cucumber, thinly sliced
⅓ cup crumbled blue cheese
¼ cup Italian dressing

1. Drain tomatoes, reserving liquid. In large skillet, cook reserved liquid until thickened, about 5 minutes, stirring occasionally.

2. Add chicken and tarragon; cook until chicken is no longer pink, stirring frequently.

3. Cool. In large bowl, toss chicken and tomato liquid with remaining ingredients. *Makes 4 servings*

Chicken Salad with Goat Cheese

Salad Vinaigrette (recipe follows)
6 cups fresh, mixed salad greens
½ small red onion, thinly sliced
1 small carrot, cut in strips
1 yellow bell pepper, cut in strips
5 ounces goat cheese, cut in 4 pieces
4 small rosemary sprigs (or basil leaves)
4 chicken breasts, halved, boned, with skins
Olive oil, as needed
Salt and pepper to taste
¼ cup pine nuts, toasted

Preheat oven broiler. Prepare vinaigrette. In a large bowl combine salad greens, onion, carrot and bell pepper; chill. Push a piece of goat cheese and sprig of rosemary between the skin and meat of each chicken breast. Smooth the skin over the meat. Brush with olive oil; season with salt and pepper.

Place chicken on broiler pan, skin side up. Broil 7 or 8 minutes per side or until breast meat is no longer pink. Toss salad with dressing; divide among 4 small plates. Place each chicken breast on a cutting board; cut into slices. Arrange on a bed of salad. Garnish with pine nuts. Serve at once.

Makes 4 servings

Salad Vinaigrette

⅓ cup olive oil
2 tablespoons balsamic vinegar or red wine vinegar
1 clove garlic, minced
Salt and pepper to taste

Whisk ingredients together.

Favorite recipe from **National Chicken Council**

Chicken Salad

¼ cup mayonnaise
¼ cup sour cream
1 tablespoon lemon juice
1 teaspoon sugar
1 teaspoon grated lemon peel
1 teaspoon Dijon mustard
½ teaspoon salt
⅛ to ¼ teaspoon white pepper
2 cups diced cooked chicken
1 cup sliced celery
¼ cup sliced green onions
Lettuce leaves
Crumbled blue cheese (optional)

Combine mayonnaise, sour cream, lemon juice, sugar, lemon peel, mustard, salt and pepper in large bowl.

Add chicken, celery and green onions; stir to combine. Cover; refrigerate at least 1 hour to allow flavors to blend.

Serve salad on lettuce-lined plate. Sprinkle with blue cheese, if desired.

Makes 4 servings

Balsamic Chicken Salad

Prep Time: 10 minutes

⅓ **cup olive oil**
¼ **cup *French's*® Honey Mustard**
2 **tablespoons balsamic or red wine vinegar**
1 **teaspoon minced shallots or onion**
8 **cups mixed salad greens, washed and torn**
1 **package (10 ounces) fully cooked carved chicken breasts**
1 **package (4 ounces) goat or Feta cheese, crumbled**
1 **cup croutons**

1. Whisk together oil, mustard, vinegar, shallots, *2 tablespoons water* and ⅛ *teaspoon salt.*

2. Arrange salad greens, chicken, cheese and croutons on serving plates. Serve with dressing.
Makes 4 servings

California Chef Salad

Prep Time: 6 to 8 minutes
Cook Time: None

1 **package (10 ounces) PERDUE® SHORT CUTS® Fresh Lemon Pepper Carved Chicken Breast**
½ **cup prepared Catalina-style dressing, divided**
1 **package (10 ounces) prewashed fresh mixed salad greens**
4 **ounces PERDUE® Turkey Ham, cut into strips**
4 **ounces sliced Swiss cheese, cut into strips**
2 **ripe tomatoes, cut into wedges**

Combine chicken with ¼ cup dressing. Place greens on four chilled dinner plates. Arrange chicken slices, ham and cheese over greens. Garnish with tomato wedges. Drizzle with remaining dressing and serve with hot, crusty sourdough rolls.
Makes 4 servings

Tip: Another choice for the salad bowl is PERDUE® Rotisserie Chicken sliced into thin strips.

Balsamic Chicken Salad

BEST-LOVED
Chicken Recipes

DOWN-HOME FAVORITES

Nutty Oven-Fried Chicken Drumsticks

**12 chicken drumsticks or 6 legs
(about 3 pounds)**
1 egg, beaten
1 cup cornflake crumbs
⅓ cup finely chopped pecans
1 tablespoon sugar
1½ teaspoons salt
½ teaspoon onion powder
½ teaspoon black pepper
**¼ cup butter or margarine,
melted**

Preheat oven to 400°F. Toss chicken legs with egg to coat.

Combine cornflakes, pecans, sugar, salt, onion powder and pepper in large resealable plastic food storage bag. Add chicken legs, two at a time; shake to coat.

Place chicken on foil-lined baking sheet; drizzle with melted butter. Bake 40 to 45 minutes or until tender.

Makes 4 to 6 servings

Creamy Herbed Chicken

1 package (9 ounces) fresh bow-tie pasta or fusilli*

1 tablespoon vegetable oil

2 boneless skinless chicken breasts, cut into halves, then cut into ½-inch strips

1 small red onion, cut into slices

1 package (10 ounces) frozen green peas, thawed and drained

1 yellow or red bell pepper, cut into strips

½ cup chicken broth

1 container (8 ounces) soft cream cheese with garlic and herbs

Salt and black pepper

Substitute dried bow-tie pasta or fusilli for fresh pasta. Cooking time will be longer; follow package directions.

Cook pasta in lightly salted boiling water according to package directions, about 5 minutes; drain.

Meanwhile, heat oil in large skillet or wok over medium-high heat. Add chicken and onion; cook and stir 3 minutes or until chicken is no longer pink in center. Add peas and bell pepper; cook and stir 4 minutes. Reduce heat to medium.

Stir in broth and cream cheese. Cook, stirring constantly, until cream cheese is melted. Combine pasta and chicken mixture in serving bowl; mix lightly. Season to taste with salt and black pepper. Garnish as desired.

Makes 4 servings

Big Easy Chicken Creole

1 package (about 2½ pounds) PERDUE® Fresh Split Skinless Chicken Breasts

1½ to 2 teaspoons Creole or Cajun seasoning

Salt to taste

2 tablespoons canola oil

½ green bell pepper, seeded and chopped (about ¾ cup)

1 small onion, peeled and chopped (about ¾ cup)

1 can (14½ ounces) Cajun- or Mexican-style tomatoes

¼ cup white wine (optional)

2 tablespoons minced fresh parsley (optional)

With sharp knife, make 3 to 4 parallel slashes in each piece of chicken. Rub with seasoning mixture and salt, getting seasonings into slashes. In large skillet over medium heat, heat oil. Add chicken and cook 5 to 6 minutes per side, until browned. Remove and set aside. Add pepper and onion to skillet; sauté 2 to 3 minutes until softened. Stir in tomatoes and wine. Return chicken to pan, meat-side down. Partially cover with lid and reduce heat to medium-low. Simmer 30 to 35 minutes, until chicken is tender and cooked through (meat thermometer inserted in thickest part of breast should register 170°F). Sprinkle with parsley; serve over hot, fluffy rice. *Makes 4 servings*

Creamy Herbed Chicken

Noodly Chicken & Green Bean Skillet

Prep Time: 5 minutes
Cook Time: 20 minutes

3 tablespoons margarine or butter, divided
¾ pound boneless, skinless chicken breasts, cut into ¾-inch pieces
1 (2.8-ounce) can French fried real onions (about 2 cups), divided
¾ cup milk
1 (4.7-ounce) package PASTA RONI® Fettuccine Alfredo
1 (14½-ounce) can French-style green beans, drained

1. In large skillet over medium-high heat, melt 1 tablespoon margarine. Add chicken; sauté 5 minutes or until chicken is no longer pink inside. Stir in 1½ cups fried onions. Remove from skillet; set aside.

2. In same skillet, bring 1¼ cups water, milk, remaining 2 tablespoons margarine, pasta and Special Seasonings to a boil. Reduce heat to low. Gently boil uncovered, 4 minutes, stirring occasionally.

3. Stir in chicken mixture and green beans; simmer 1 to 2 minutes or until pasta is tender, stirring frequently. Top with remaining fried onions.

Makes 4 servings

Baked Barbecue Chicken

1 cut-up whole chicken (about 3 pounds)
1 small onion, cut into slices
1½ cups ketchup
½ cup packed brown sugar
¼ cup Worcestershire sauce
2 tablespoons lemon juice
1 tablespoon liquid smoke

Preheat oven to 375°F. Place chicken in 13×9-inch baking dish coated with nonstick cooking spray. Arrange onion slices over top.

Combine ketchup, brown sugar, Worcestershire sauce, lemon juice and liquid smoke in small saucepan. Heat over medium heat 2 to 3 minutes or until sugar dissolves. Pour over chicken.

Bake chicken 1 hour or until juices run clear. Discard onion slices. Let stand 10 minutes before serving.

Makes 6 servings

Serving Suggestion: Serve with baked potatoes, crusty French bread and tossed green salad.

Baked Barbecue Chicken

Rocky Mountain Hash with Smoked Chicken

1½ **pounds Colorado russet variety potatoes, unpeeled**
2 **tablespoons olive oil, divided**
1 **teaspoon salt, divided**
¼ **teaspoon black pepper**
  Nonstick cooking spray
2 **cups chopped red or yellow onions**
2 **tablespoons bottled minced garlic**
2 **cups diced red bell pepper**
⅛ **to ¼ teaspoon cayenne pepper**
2 **cups shredded smoked chicken or turkey**
1 **can (11 ounces) whole kernel corn**

Cut potatoes into ½- to ¾-inch chunks. Toss with 1 tablespoon oil, ½ teaspoon salt and black pepper. Spray 15×10×1-inch baking pan with nonstick cooking spray. Arrange potato chunks in single layer; roast at 450°F for 20 to 30 minutes or until tender, stirring and tossing occasionally. In large skillet heat remaining 1 tablespoon oil. Sauté onions and garlic until tender. Add red bell pepper, remaining ½ teaspoon salt and cayenne pepper. Cook and stir until peppers are crisp-tender. Stir in chicken, corn and potatoes. Cook and stir until heated through.

Makes 6 to 8 servings

Favorite recipe from **Colorado Potato Administrative Committee**

Honey Baked Chicken

1 **cup dry bread crumbs**
3 **tablespoons cornmeal**
1 **tablespoon LAWRY'S® Seasoned Salt**
2 **teaspoons LAWRY'S® Garlic Powder with Parsley**
¼ **teaspoon cayenne pepper**
3 **tablespoons honey**
3 **tablespoons Dijon-style mustard**
2 **tablespoons water**
2½ **to 3 pounds chicken fryer pieces**

In medium bowl, combine bread crumbs, cornmeal, Seasoned Salt, Garlic Powder with Parsley and cayenne pepper; mix well and set aside. In small bowl, combine honey, mustard and water; mix well. Dip chicken pieces in honey mixture, then in bread crumbs. Place in 13×9×2-inch baking dish. Bake, uncovered, in 375°F oven 45 to 50 minutes until chicken is no longer pink in center and juices run clear when cut (175°-180°F at thickest joint).

Makes 6 to 8 servings

Serving Suggestion: Serve with steamed carrots and peas or broccoli and mushrooms.

Baked Chicken with Crispy Cheese-Garlic Crust

1 teaspoon olive oil
½ cup chopped garlic (one large head)
4 tablespoons water, divided
½ cup dry bread crumbs
¼ cup Dijon mustard (or more to taste)
1 cup (4 ounces) shredded JARLSBERG Cheese
3 pounds chicken pieces, skin removed and trimmed of fat

Preheat oven to 400°F. Heat oil in large skillet over high heat. Add garlic; cook and stir 2 minutes. Add 2 tablespoons water; cover tightly. Reduce heat to low; cook 4 minutes.

Meanwhile, mix crumbs and mustard. Add garlic and blend well. Add cheese plus remaining 2 tablespoons water and mix to make a paste.

Arrange chicken on rack in foil-lined baking pan. Pat thin layer of garlic-cheese paste on top side of chicken pieces to form a crust. Bake, loosely tented with foil, 1 hour or until juices run clear when pierced with a knife.

Makes 3 to 4 servings

Kahlúa® Stir-Fry Chicken

1½ pounds boneless skinless chicken, cut into ½-inch pieces
2 tablespoons beaten egg
¼ cup plus 2 tablespoons vegetable oil, divided
2 tablespoons plus 1 teaspoon cornstarch, divided
½ cup water chestnuts, sliced
6 asparagus tips, fresh or frozen
1 green bell pepper, cut into ½-inch strips
4 ounces mushrooms, sliced
4 ounces snow peas
3 tablespoons KAHLÚA® Liqueur
1 cup cashews
3 green onions, chopped

Coat chicken in mixture of egg, 2 tablespoons oil and 2 tablespoons cornstarch. Heat remaining ¼ cup oil in wok or skillet. Add chicken. Cook until golden brown; remove and drain well. Remove all but 2 tablespoons oil from wok; heat. Add all vegetables except green onions. Stir-fry 3 to 5 minutes. Combine Kahlúa® and remaining 1 teaspoon cornstarch; add to vegetables. Bring to a boil, then simmer to slightly thicken. Add chicken and cashews; heat thoroughly. Remove to serving platter. Garnish with green onions.

Makes 4 to 6 servings

Southern-Style Chicken and Greens

1 teaspoon salt
1 teaspoon paprika
½ teaspoon black pepper
3½ pounds chicken pieces
4 thick slices smoked bacon (4 ounces), cut crosswise into ¼-inch strips
1 cup uncooked rice
1 can (14½ ounces) stewed tomatoes, undrained
1¼ cups chicken broth
2 cups packed coarsely chopped fresh collard or mustard greens or kale (3 to 4 ounces)

Preheat oven to 350°F.

Combine salt, paprika and pepper in small bowl. Sprinkle meaty side of chicken pieces with salt mixture; set aside.

Place bacon in ovenproof Dutch oven; cook over medium heat until crisp. Remove from Dutch oven; drain on paper towels. Reserve drippings.

Heat drippings in Dutch oven over medium-high heat until hot. Arrange chicken in single layer in Dutch oven and cook 3 minutes per side or until chicken is browned. Transfer to plate; set aside. Repeat with remaining pieces. Reserve 1 tablespoon drippings in Dutch oven.

Add rice to drippings; cook and stir 1 minute. Add tomatoes with juice, broth, collard greens and half of bacon; bring to a boil over high heat. Remove from heat; arrange chicken over rice mixture.

Bake, covered, about 40 minutes or until chicken is no longer pink in centers and most of liquid is absorbed. Let stand 5 minutes before serving. Transfer to serving platter; sprinkle with remaining bacon.

Makes 4 to 6 servings

Serving Suggestion: Serve with corn bread or corn muffins.

Bacon & Cheese Stuffed Chicken

Prep Time: 15 minutes
Cook Time: 30 minutes

4 boneless, skinless chicken breast halves (about 1¼ pounds), pounded ¼ inch thick
1 cup shredded mozzarella cheese (about 4 ounces)
4 slices bacon, crisp-cooked and crumbled
1 egg, slightly beaten
½ cup Italian seasoned dry bread crumbs
2 tablespoons olive or vegetable oil
1 jar (26 to 28 ounces) RAGÚ® Hearty Robusto!™ Pasta Sauce
1 cup chicken broth
8 ounces linguine or spaghetti, cooked and drained

1. Evenly top each chicken breast half with cheese and bacon. Roll up and secure with wooden toothpicks. Dip chicken in egg, then bread crumbs.

2. In 12-inch nonstick skillet, heat oil over medium heat and brown chicken, turning occasionally. Stir in Ragú Pasta Sauce and broth. Bring to a boil over high heat. Reduce heat to low and simmer covered 10 minutes or until chicken is no longer pink.

3. To serve, arrange chicken and sauce over hot linguine. Garnish, if desired, with chopped fresh basil or parsley. *Makes 4 servings*

Spicy Fried Chicken

⅓ cup all-purpose flour
2 tablespoons cornmeal
1 teaspoon baking powder
1 package (1.0 ounces) LAWRY'S® Taco Spices & Seasonings
1¼ teaspoons LAWRY'S® Seasoned Salt
1 teaspoon paprika
¾ teaspoon cayenne pepper
½ teaspoon LAWRY'S® Seasoned Pepper
3 to 3½ pounds chicken pieces
¼ cup butter or shortening, melted
2 tablespoons lemon juice

In large resealable plastic food storage bag, combine flour, cornmeal, baking powder, Taco Spices & Seasonings, Seasoned Salt, paprika, cayenne pepper and Seasoned Pepper; mix well. Add chicken, a few pieces at a time, to plastic bag; seal bag. Shake until well coated. Place chicken in shallow baking pan. Combine butter and lemon juice; drizzle over chicken. Bake in 400°F oven 1 hour or until chicken is no longer pink in center.
Makes 6 to 8 servings

Serving Suggestion: Serve with hot buttered corn on the cob and lots of napkins.

Bacon & Cheese Stuffed Chicken

Swiss 'n' Chicken Casserole

Prep Time: 20 minutes
Cook Time: 40 minutes

4 cups chopped cooked chicken
2 cups KRAFT® Shredded Swiss Cheese
2 cups croutons
2 cups sliced celery
1 cup MIRACLE WHIP® or MIRACLE WHIP® LIGHT Dressing
½ cup milk
¼ cup chopped onion
Chopped walnuts (optional)

• Heat oven to 350°F.

• Mix all ingredients. Spoon into 2-quart casserole. Sprinkle with walnuts, if desired.

• Bake 40 minutes or until thoroughly heated.   *Makes 6 servings*

Garlicky Baked Chicken

1½ cups fresh bread crumbs
3 cloves garlic, minced
1 tablespoon peanut or vegetable oil
2 tablespoons soy sauce
1 tablespoon Chinese hot mustard
1 cut-up whole chicken (about 3½ pounds) *or* 3½ pounds chicken parts, skinned, if desired

1. Preheat oven to 350°F. Combine bread crumbs, garlic and oil in shallow dish.

2. Combine soy sauce and hot mustard in small bowl; brush evenly over chicken. Dip chicken in bread crumb mixture to coat lightly, but evenly. Place on foil-lined baking sheet.

3. Bake chicken 45 to 55 minutes or until juices run clear.
Makes 4 to 6 servings

Chicken with Brandied Fruit Sauce

4 boneless, skinless chicken
  breast halves
½ teaspoon salt
¼ teaspoon ground nutmeg
2 tablespoons butter or
  margarine
1 tablespoon cornstarch
¼ teaspoon ground red pepper
  Juice of 1 orange
  Juice of 1 lemon
  Juice of 1 lime
⅓ cup orange marmalade
2 tablespoons brandy
1 cup red seedless grapes

Pound chicken to ½-inch thickness on hard surface with meat mallet or rolling pin. Sprinkle salt and nutmeg over chicken. Heat butter in large skillet over medium-high heat. Add chicken and cook, turning, about 8 minutes or until chicken is brown, fork-tender and no longer pink in center. Mix cornstarch and red pepper in small bowl. Stir in orange juice, lemon juice and lime juice; set aside. Remove chicken to serving platter. Add marmalade to same skillet; heat until melted. Stir in juice mixture; cook and stir until mixture boils and thickens. Add brandy and grapes. Return chicken to pan; spoon sauce over chicken. Cook over low heat 5 minutes.   *Makes 4 servings*

Favorite recipe from **Delmarva Poultry Industry, Inc.**

Pennsylvania Dutch Chicken Bake

1 package (about 1¾ pounds)
  PERDUE® Fresh Skinless
  Chicken Thighs
  Salt and pepper to taste
1 to 2 tablespoons canola oil
1 can (14 to 16 ounces)
  sauerkraut, undrained
1 can (14 to 15 ounces) whole
  onions, drained
1 tart red apple, unpeeled and
  sliced
6 to 8 dried whole apricots
½ cup raisins
¼ cup brown sugar, or to taste

Preheat oven to 350°F. Season thighs with salt and pepper. In large nonstick skillet over medium-high heat, heat oil. Cook thighs 6 to 8 minutes per side until browned. Meanwhile, in 12×9-inch shallow baking dish, mix sauerkraut, onions, apple, apricots, raisins and brown sugar until blended. Arrange thighs in sauerkraut mixture. Cover and bake 30 to 40 minutes or until chicken is cooked through and a meat thermometer inserted in thickest part of thigh registers 180°F.

Makes 6 servings

Pepper Glazed Cajun Chicken

4 boneless, skinless chicken breast halves
½ to 1 teaspoon Cajun seasoning*
1 tablespoon vegetable oil
¼ cup sliced green onions
6 tablespoons hot pepper jelly
¼ cup defatted chicken broth
2 tablespoons white vinegar

Use larger measurement if hotter flavor is preferred.

Sprinkle Cajun seasoning over chicken. Heat oil in large nonstick skillet over medium-high heat. Add chicken; cook about 10 minutes or until chicken is brown, turning occasionally. Remove chicken and set aside. Add onions to drippings in skillet; cook and stir 2 minutes. Add jelly, broth and vinegar; cook and stir until jelly melts.

Return chicken to pan; spoon glaze over chicken. Cover and cook over medium-low heat about 5 minutes or until chicken is fork-tender and no longer pink in center, turning occasionally.

Remove chicken to serving platter. Increase heat to medium-high and cook until glaze thickens slightly. Spoon glaze over chicken.

Makes 4 servings

Favorite recipe from **Delmarva Poultry Industry, Inc.**

Country Chicken Pot Pie

Prep Time: 5 minutes
Cook Time: 15 minutes

1 package (1.8 ounces) white sauce mix
2¼ cups milk
2 to 3 cups diced cooked chicken*
3 cups BIRDS EYE® frozen Mixed Vegetables
1½ cups seasoned croutons**

No leftover cooked chicken handy? Before beginning recipe, cut 1 pound boneless skinless chicken into 1-inch cubes. Brown chicken in 1 tablespoon butter or margarine in large skillet, then proceed with recipe.

**For a quick homemade touch, substitute 4 bakery-bought biscuits for croutons. Split and add to skillet, cut side down.*

• Prepare white sauce mix with milk in large skillet according to package directions.

• Add chicken and vegetables. Bring to boil over medium-high heat; cook 3 minutes or until heated through, stirring occasionally.

• Top with croutons; cover and let stand 5 minutes.

Makes about 4 servings

Serving Suggestion: Serve with a green salad.

Pepper Glazed Cajun Chicken

Hidden Valley Fried Chicken

1 broiler-fryer chicken, cut up
   (2 to 2½ pounds)
1 cup prepared HIDDEN VALLEY®
   Original Ranch® Salad
   Dressing
¾ cup all-purpose flour
1 teaspoon salt
½ teaspoon freshly ground black
   pepper
   Vegetable oil

Place chicken pieces in shallow baking dish; pour salad dressing over chicken. Cover; refrigerate at least 8 hours. Remove chicken. Shake off excess marinade; discard marinade. Preheat oven to 350°F. On plate, mix flour, salt and pepper; roll chicken in seasoned flour. Heat ½ inch oil in large skillet until small cube of bread dropped into oil browns in 60 seconds or until oil is 375°F. Fry chicken until golden, 5 to 7 minutes on each side; transfer to baking pan. Bake until chicken is tender and juices run clear, about 30 minutes. Serve with corn muffins, if desired.

Makes 4 main-dish servings

Hidden Valley Fried Chicken

Classic Chicken Biscuit Pie

12 boneless, skinless chicken
    tenderloins, cut into 1-inch
    pieces
4 cups water
2 boxes UNCLE BEN'S® COUNTRY
    INN® Chicken Flavored Rice
1 can (10¾ ounces) condensed
    cream of chicken soup
1 bag (1 pound) frozen peas,
    potatoes and carrots
1 container (12 ounces)
    refrigerated buttermilk
    biscuits

1. Heat oven to 400°F. In large saucepan, combine chicken, water, rice, contents of seasoning packets, soup and vegetable mixture; mix well. Bring to a boil. Cover; reduce heat and simmer 10 minutes.

2. Place in 13×9-inch baking pan; top with biscuits.

3. Bake 10 to 12 minutes or until biscuits are golden brown.
Makes 8 to 10 servings

Cook's Tip: For individual pot pies, place rice mixture in small ramekins or casseroles. Proceed with recipe as directed.

Honey Mustard BBQ Chicken Stir-Fry

Prep Time: 10 minutes
Cook Time: 15 minutes

1 box (10 ounces) couscous
    pasta
1 pound boneless chicken, cut
    into strips
1 medium red bell pepper, cut
    into thin strips
1 medium onion, sliced
⅓ cup *French's*® Honey Mustard
⅓ cup barbecue sauce

1. Prepare couscous according to package directions. Keep warm.

2. Heat *1 tablespoon oil* in large nonstick skillet over medium-high heat. Stir-fry chicken in batches 5 to 10 minutes or until browned. Transfer to bowl. Drain fat.

3. Heat *1 tablespoon oil* in same skillet until hot. Stir-fry vegetables 3 minutes or until crisp-tender. Return chicken to skillet. Stir in ⅔ *cup water,* mustard and barbecue sauce. Heat to boiling, stirring often. Serve over couscous.
Makes 4 servings

BEST-LOVED
Chicken Recipes

INTERNATIONAL FLAVORS

Asian Chicken and Noodles

Prep Time: *5 minutes*
Cook Time: *20 minutes*

1 package (3 ounces) chicken flavor instant ramen noodles
1 bag (16 ounces) BIRDS EYE® frozen Farm Fresh Mixtures Broccoli, Carrots and Water Chestnuts*
1 tablespoon vegetable oil
1 pound boneless skinless chicken breasts, cut into thin strips
¼ cup stir-fry sauce

*Or, substitute 1 bag (16 ounces) Birds Eye® frozen Broccoli Cuts.

• Reserve seasoning packet from noodles.

• Bring 2 cups water to boil in large saucepan. Add noodles and vegetables. Cook 3 minutes, stirring occasionally; drain.

• Meanwhile, heat oil in large nonstick skillet over medium-high heat. Add chicken; cook and stir until browned, about 8 minutes.

• Stir in noodles, vegetables, stir-fry sauce and reserved seasoning packet; heat through.
Makes about 4 servings

Citrus Chicken

1 large orange
1 large lime*
¾ cup WISH-BONE® Italian
Dressing
2½ to 3 pounds chicken pieces

*Substitution: Omit lime peel. Use 3 tablespoons lime juice.

From the orange, grate enough peel to measure 1½ teaspoons and squeeze enough juice to measure ⅓ cup; set aside.

From the lime, grate enough peel to measure 1 teaspoon and squeeze enough juice to measure 3 tablespoons; set aside.

For marinade, combine Italian dressing, orange and lime juices and orange and lime peels. In large, shallow nonaluminum baking dish or plastic bag, pour ¾ cup marinade over chicken; turn to coat. Cover, or close bag, and marinate in refrigerator, turning occasionally, 3 to 24 hours. Refrigerate remaining ½ cup marinade.

Remove chicken from marinade, discarding marinade. Grill or broil chicken, turning once and brushing frequently with refrigerated marinade, until chicken is no longer pink.

Makes 4 servings

Variation: Also terrific with WISH-BONE® Robusto Italian or Just 2 Good Italian Dressing.

Chicken Vesuvio

1 whole chicken
(about 3¾ pounds)
¼ cup olive oil
3 tablespoons lemon juice
4 cloves garlic, minced
3 large baking potatoes
Salt and lemon pepper

Preheat oven to 375°F. Place chicken, breast side down, on rack in large shallow roasting pan. Combine olive oil, lemon juice and garlic; brush half of oil mixture over chicken. Set aside remaining oil mixture. Roast chicken, uncovered, 30 minutes.

Meanwhile, peel potatoes; cut lengthwise into quarters. Turn chicken, breast side up. Arrange potatoes around chicken in roasting pan. Brush chicken and potatoes with remaining oil mixture; sprinkle with salt and lemon pepper seasoning to taste. Roast chicken and potatoes, basting occasionally with pan juices, 50 minutes or until meat thermometer inserted into thickest part of chicken thigh, not touching bone, registers 180°F and potatoes are tender.

Makes 4 to 6 servings

Chicken Vesuvio

Jerk Chicken and Pasta

Jerk Sauce (recipe follows)
12 ounces boneless skinless chicken breasts
Nonstick cooking spray
1 cup canned fat-free reduced-sodium chicken broth
1 green bell pepper, sliced
2 green onions with tops, sliced
8 ounces uncooked fettuccine, cooked and kept warm
Grated Parmesan cheese (optional)

1. Spread Jerk Sauce on both sides of chicken. Place in glass dish; refrigerate, covered, 15 to 30 minutes.

2. Spray medium skillet with cooking spray. Heat over medium heat until hot. Add chicken; cook 5 to 10 minutes or until browned and no longer pink in center. Add chicken broth, bell pepper and onions; bring to a boil. Reduce heat and simmer, uncovered, 5 to 7 minutes or until vegetables are crisp-tender and broth is reduced to thin sauce consistency.

3. Remove chicken from skillet and cut into slices. Toss fettuccine, chicken and vegetable mixture in large serving bowl. Sprinkle with Parmesan cheese, if desired.

Makes 4 main-dish servings

Jerk Sauce

¼ cup loosely packed fresh cilantro
2 tablespoons coarsely chopped fresh ginger
2 tablespoons black pepper
2 tablespoons lime juice
3 cloves garlic
1 tablespoon ground allspice
½ teaspoon curry powder
¼ teaspoon ground cloves
⅛ teaspoon ground red pepper

Combine all ingredients in food processor or blender; process until thick paste consistency.

Makes about ¼ cup

Grilled Italian Chicken

½ cup prepared HIDDEN VALLEY® Ranch Italian Salad Dressing
1 tablespoon Dijon-style mustard
4 boned chicken breast halves

In small bowl or measuring cup, whisk together salad dressing and mustard; reserve 3 tablespoons for final baste. Brush chicken generously with some of remaining dressing mixture. Grill or broil, basting several times with dressing mixture, until chicken is golden and cooked through, about 5 minutes on each side. Brush generously with reserved dressing just before removing from grill.

Makes 4 servings

Jerk Chicken and Pasta

Classic Chicken Parmesan

6 boneless, skinless chicken breast halves, pounded thin (about 1½ pounds)
2 eggs, slightly beaten
1 cup Italian seasoned dry bread crumbs
2 tablespoons olive or vegetable oil
1 jar (26 to 28 ounces) RAGÚ® Old World Style® Pasta Sauce
1 cup shredded mozzarella cheese (about 4 ounces)

Preheat oven to 375°F. Dip chicken in eggs, then bread crumbs, coating well.

In 12-inch skillet, heat oil over medium-high heat and brown chicken; drain on paper towels.

In 11×7-inch baking dish, evenly spread 1 cup Ragú® Old World Style Pasta Sauce. Arrange chicken in dish, then top with remaining sauce. Sprinkle with mozzarella cheese and, if desired, grated Parmesan cheese. Bake 25 minutes or until chicken is no longer pink. *Makes 6 servings*

Recipe Tip: To pound chicken, place a boneless, skinless breast between two sheets of waxed paper. Use a rolling pin to press down and out from the center to flatten.

Kung Pao Chicken

1 pound boneless, skinless chicken breasts, cut into 1-inch pieces
1 tablespoon cornstarch
2 teaspoons CRISCO® Oil*
3 tablespoons chopped green onions with tops
2 cloves garlic, minced
¼ to 1½ teaspoons crushed red pepper
¼ to ½ teaspoon ground ginger
¼ cup rice vinegar
¼ cup soy sauce
1 tablespoon sugar
⅓ cup unsalted dry roasted peanuts
4 cups hot cooked rice (cooked without salt or fat)

Use your favorite Crisco Oil product.

1. Combine chicken and cornstarch in small bowl; toss. Heat oil in large skillet or wok on medium-high heat. Add chicken. Stir-fry 5 to 7 minutes or until no longer pink in center. Remove from skillet. Add onions, garlic, red pepper and ginger to skillet. Stir-fry 15 seconds. Remove from heat.

2. Combine vinegar, soy sauce and sugar in small bowl. Stir well. Add to skillet. Return chicken to skillet. Stir until coated. Stir in nuts. Heat thoroughly, stirring occasionally. Serve over hot rice. *Makes 4 servings*

Chicken Burritos

1 package (8) ORTEGA® Burrito
    Dinner Kit (flour tortillas and
    burrito seasoning mix)
1 tablespoon vegetable oil
1 pound (3 to 4) boneless,
    skinless chicken breast
    halves, cut into 2-inch strips
1½ cups water
    Toppings: shredded Cheddar
    cheese, shredded iceberg
    lettuce, chopped green
    onions, sliced ripe olives and
    ORTEGA® Thick & Chunky
    Salsa, hot, medium or mild

HEAT oil in large skillet over medium-high heat. Add chicken. Cook for 3 to 4 minutes or until no longer pink in center. Add burrito seasoning mix and water. Bring to a boil. Reduce heat to low; cook, stirring occasionally, for 5 to 6 minutes or until mixture is thickened.

REMOVE tortillas from outer plastic pouch. Microwave on HIGH (100%) power for 10 to 15 seconds or until warm. Or heat each tortilla, turning frequently, in small skillet over medium-high heat until warm.

SPREAD chicken mixture over tortillas. Top with cheese, lettuce, green onions, olives and salsa. Fold into burritos. *Makes 8 burritos*

Polynesian Chicken and Rice

Prep Time: 20 minutes
Cook Time: 10 minutes

1 can (20 ounces) DOLE®
    Pineapple Tidbits or
    Pineapple Chunks
½ cup DOLE® Seedless or Golden
    Raisins
½ cup sliced green onions
2 teaspoons finely chopped fresh
    ginger *or* ½ teaspoon ground
    ginger
1 clove garlic, finely chopped
3 cups cooked white or brown
    rice
2 cups chopped cooked chicken
    breast or turkey breast
2 tablespoons low-sodium soy
    sauce

• Drain pineapple; reserve 4 tablespoons juice.

• Heat 2 tablespoons reserved juice over medium heat in large, nonstick skillet. Add raisins, green onions, ginger and garlic; cook and stir 3 minutes.

• Stir in pineapple, rice, chicken, soy sauce and remaining 2 tablespoons juice. Cover; reduce heat to low and cook 5 minutes more or until heated through. Garnish with cherry tomatoes and green onions, if desired.
Makes 4 servings

Chicken Marsala

6 ounces uncooked broad egg noodles
½ cup Italian-style bread crumbs
1 teaspoon dried basil leaves
1 egg
1 teaspoon water
4 boneless skinless chicken breast halves
3 tablespoons olive oil, divided
¾ cup chopped onion
8 ounces button mushrooms, sliced
3 cloves garlic, minced
3 tablespoons all-purpose flour
1 can (14½ ounces) chicken broth
½ cup dry marsala wine
¾ teaspoon salt
¾ teaspoon black pepper
Chopped fresh parsley

Preheat oven to 375°F. Spray 11X7-inch baking dish with nonstick cooking spray. Cook noodles according to package directions; drain and place in prepared dish.

Meanwhile, combine bread crumbs and basil on shallow plate. Beat egg with water in medium bowl. Dip chicken in egg mixture; then roll in crumb mixture, patting to coat. Heat 2 tablespoons oil in large skillet over medium heat until hot. Cook chicken 3 minutes per side or until browned; set aside.

Heat remaining 1 tablespoon oil in same skillet over medium heat. Add onion; cook and stir 5 minutes. Add mushrooms and garlic; cook and stir 3 minutes. Sprinkle flour over onion mixture; cook and stir 1 minute. Add broth, wine, salt and pepper; bring to a boil over high heat. Cook and stir 5 minutes or until sauce thickens. Reserve ½ cup sauce. Pour remaining sauce over noodles; stir until noodles are well coated. Place chicken on top of noodles. Spoon reserved sauce over chicken.

Bake uncovered, 20 minutes or until chicken is no longer pink in center. Sprinkle with parsley.

Makes 4 servings

Simple Stir-Fry

1 tablespoon vegetable oil
12 boneless, skinless chicken tenderloins, cut into 1-inch pieces
1 bag (1 pound) frozen stir-fry vegetable mix
2 tablespoons soy sauce
2 tablespoons honey
2 (2-cup) bags UNCLE BEN'S® Boil-in-Bag Rice

1. Heat oil in large skillet or wok. Add chicken; cook over medium-high heat 6 to 8 minutes or until lightly browned. Add vegetables, soy sauce and honey. Cover and cook 5 to 8 minutes or until chicken is no longer pink in center and vegetables are crisp-tender.

2. Meanwhile, cook rice according to package directions. Serve stir-fry over rice. *Makes 4 servings*

Chicken di Napolitano

1 tablespoon olive oil
2 boneless, skinless chicken breasts (about 8 ounces)
1 can (14½ ounces) diced tomatoes, undrained
1¼ cups water
1 box UNCLE BEN'S® Rice Pilaf
¼ cup chopped fresh basil or 1½ teaspoons dried basil leaves

1. Heat oil in large skillet. Add chicken, cook over medium-high heat 8 to 10 minutes or until lightly browned on both sides.

2. Add tomatoes, water, rice and contents of seasoning packet. Bring to a boil. Cover; reduce heat and simmer 15 to 18 minutes or until chicken is no longer pink in center and liquid is absorbed.

3. Stir in basil. Slice chicken and serve over rice.   *Makes 2 servings*

Cook's Tip: For more flavor, substitute diced tomatoes with Italian herbs or roasted garlic for diced tomatoes.

Spanish Skillet Supper

Prep Time: 5 minutes
Cook Time: 20 minutes

1 tablespoon vegetable oil
1 pound boneless skinless chicken breasts, cut into 1-inch cubes
2 cups hot water
1 package (4.4 ounces) Spanish rice and sauce mix
2 cups BIRDS EYE® frozen Green Peas
Crushed red pepper flakes

• Heat oil in large skillet over medium-high heat. Add chicken; cook and stir until lightly browned, about 5 minutes.

• Add hot water, rice and sauce mix; bring to boil. Reduce heat to medium-low; simmer, uncovered, 5 minutes.

• Stir in green peas; increase heat to medium-high. Cover and cook 5 minutes or until peas and rice are tender.

• Sprinkle with red pepper flakes.
         Makes about 4 servings

Grilled Chicken with Asian Pesto

**4 boneless skinless chicken
breast halves *or* 8 boneless
skinless thighs *or* combination
of both
Olive or vegetable oil
Salt and black pepper
Asian Pesto (recipe follows)
Lime wedges**

Place chicken between two pieces of waxed paper; pound to ⅜-inch thickness. Brush chicken with oil; season to taste with salt and pepper. Spread about ½ tablespoon Asian Pesto on both sides of each breast or thigh.

Oil hot grid to help prevent sticking. Grill chicken, on an uncovered grill, over medium KINGSFORD® Briquets, 6 to 8 minutes until chicken is cooked through, turning once. Serve with additional Asian Pesto and lime wedges. *Makes 4 servings*

Asian Pesto

**1 cup packed fresh basil
1 cup packed fresh cilantro
1 cup packed fresh mint leaves
¼ cup olive or vegetable oil
2 cloves garlic, chopped
2½ to 3½ tablespoons lime juice
1 tablespoon sugar
1 teaspoon salt
1 teaspoon black pepper**

Combine all ingredients in a blender or food processor; process until smooth. *Makes about ¾ cup*

Note: The Asian Pesto recipe makes enough for 6 servings. Leftovers can be saved and used as a spread for sandwiches.

Chicken with Roasted Garlic Marinara

Prep: 10 minutes
Cook: 5 minutes

**1 package (9 ounces)
DI GIORNO® Angel's Hair
1 package (6 ounces) LOUIS
RICH® Italian Style or Grilled
Chicken Breast Strips
1 package (10 ounces)
DI GIORNO® Roasted Garlic
Marinara Sauce
DI GIORNO® Shredded
Parmesan Cheese**

PREPARE pasta as directed on package; drain.

MIX chicken breast strips and sauce in saucepan. Cook on medium heat 5 minutes or until thoroughly heated.

SERVE over pasta; sprinkle with cheese. *Makes 3 to 4 servings*

Chicken Walnut Stir-Fry

Sauce
- ⅔ cup chicken broth
- 1½ tablespoons LA CHOY® Soy Sauce
- 1 tablespoon *each:* cornstarch and dry sherry
- ½ teaspoon sugar
- ¼ teaspoon *each:* pepper and Oriental sesame oil

Chicken and Vegetables
- 2 tablespoons cornstarch
- 2 teaspoons LA CHOY® Soy Sauce
- 2 teaspoons dry sherry
- 1 pound boneless skinless chicken breasts, cut into thin 2-inch strips
- 4 tablespoons WESSON® Oil, divided
- 2½ cups fresh broccoli flowerettes
- 1½ teaspoons minced fresh garlic
- 1 teaspoon minced ginger root
- 1 (8-ounce) can LA CHOY® Bamboo Shoots, drained
- 1 cup toasted chopped walnuts
- 1 (6-ounce) package frozen pea pods, thawed and drained
- 1 (5-ounce) can LA CHOY® Chow Mein Noodles

In small bowl, combine sauce ingredients; set aside. In separate small bowl, combine cornstarch, soy sauce and sherry; mix well. Add chicken; toss gently to coat. In large nonstick skillet or wok, heat 3 tablespoons Wesson Oil. Add half of chicken mixture; stir-fry until chicken is no longer pink in center. Remove chicken from skillet; set aside. Repeat with remaining chicken mixture. Heat remaining 1 tablespoon Wesson Oil in same skillet. Add broccoli, garlic and ginger; stir-fry until broccoli is crisp-tender. Return chicken mixture to skillet with bamboo shoots, walnuts and pea pods; heat thoroughly, stirring occasionally. Stir sauce; add to skillet. Cook, stirring constantly, until sauce is thick and bubbly. Garnish with La Choy Chow Mein Noodles, if desired. *Makes 4 to 6 servings*

Mandarin Orange Chicken

- ½ (6-ounce) can frozen orange juice concentrate, thawed
- ⅓ cup HOLLAND HOUSE® White Cooking Wine
- ¼ cup orange marmalade
- ½ teaspoon ground ginger
- 4 boneless chicken breast halves, skinned (about 1 pound)
- 1 (11-ounce) can mandarin orange segments, drained
- ½ cup green grapes, halved

Heat oven to 350°F. In 12×8-inch (2-quart) baking dish, combine concentrate, cooking wine, marmalade and ginger; mix well. Add chicken; turn to coat. Bake at 350°F for 45 to 60 minutes, or until chicken is tender and no longer pink, basting occasionally and adding orange segments and grapes during last 5 minutes of cooking.

Makes 4 servings

Chicken Walnut Stir-Fry

Spicy Mango Chicken

¼ cup mango nectar
¼ cup chopped fresh cilantro
2 jalapeño chile peppers,
   seeded and finely chopped
2 teaspoons vegetable oil
2 teaspoons LAWRY'S® Seasoned
   Salt
½ teaspoon LAWRY'S® Garlic
   Powder with Parsley
½ teaspoon ground cumin
4 boneless, skinless chicken
   breast halves (about
   1 pound)
   Mango & Black Bean Salsa
   (recipe follows)

In small bowl, combine all ingredients except chicken and salsa; mix well. Brush marinade on both sides of chicken. Grill or broil chicken 10 to 15 minutes or until no longer pink in center and juices run clear when cut, turning once and basting often with additional marinade. *Do not baste during last 5 minutes of cooking.* Discard any remaining marinade. Top chicken with Mango & Black Bean Salsa. *Makes 4 servings*

Hint: Jalapeño peppers can sting and irritate the skin; wear rubber gloves when handling peppers and do not touch eyes.

Mango & Black Bean Salsa

1 ripe mango, peeled, seeded
   and chopped
1 cup canned black beans,
   rinsed and drained
½ cup chopped tomato
2 thinly sliced green onions
1 tablespoon chopped fresh
   cilantro
1½ teaspoons lime juice
1½ teaspoons red wine vinegar
½ teaspoon LAWRY'S® Seasoned
   Salt

In medium bowl, combine all ingredients; mix well. Let stand 30 minutes to allow flavors to blend.
Makes about 2¾ cups

Serving Suggestion: Serve with chicken or fish.

Spicy Mango Chicken

BEST-LOVED
Chicken Recipes

HOT OFF THE GRILL

Hot 'n' Spicy Chicken Barbecue

½ cup A.1.® Steak Sauce
½ cup tomato sauce
¼ cup finely chopped onion
2 tablespoons cider vinegar
2 tablespoons maple syrup
1 tablespoon vegetable oil
2 teaspoons chili powder
½ teaspoon crushed red pepper
    flakes
1 (3-pound) chicken, cut up

Blend steak sauce, tomato sauce, onion, vinegar, maple syrup, oil, chili powder and red pepper flakes in medium saucepan. Heat mixture to a boil over medium heat; reduce heat. Simmer for 5 to 7 minutes or until thickened; cool.

Grill chicken over medium heat for 30 to 40 minutes or until done, turning and basting frequently with prepared sauce. Serve hot.

Makes 4 servings

Grilled Chicken and Apple with Fresh Rosemary

½ cup apple juice
¼ cup white wine vinegar
¼ cup vegetable oil or light olive oil
1 tablespoon chopped fresh rosemary *or* 1 teaspoon dried rosemary leaves, crushed
¼ teaspoon salt
¼ teaspoon ground black pepper
3 boneless skinless chicken breasts, halved
2 Washington Golden Delicious apples, cored and sliced into ½-inch-thick rings

1. Combine juice, vinegar, oil, rosemary, salt and pepper in shallow baking dish or bowl. Add chicken and apples; marinate in refrigerator at least 30 minutes.

2. Heat grill. Remove chicken and apples from marinade; arrange on hot grill. Discard marinade. Cook chicken 20 minutes or until cooked through, turning to grill both sides. Cook and turn apples about 6 minutes or until crisp-tender. Serve.

Makes 6 servings

Favorite recipe from **Washington Apple Commission**

Lime-Mustard Marinated Chicken

2 boneless skinless chicken breast halves (about 3 ounces each)
¼ cup fresh lime juice
3 tablespoons honey mustard, divided
2 teaspoons olive oil
¼ teaspoon ground cumin
⅛ teaspoon ground red pepper
¾ cup plus 2 tablespoons chicken broth, divided
¼ cup uncooked rice
1 cup broccoli florets
⅓ cup matchstick carrots

1. Place chicken in resealable plastic food storage bag. Whisk together lime juice, 2 tablespoons mustard, olive oil, cumin and red pepper. Pour over chicken. Seal bag. Marinate in refrigerator 2 hours.

2. Combine ¾ cup chicken broth, rice and remaining 1 tablespoon mustard in small saucepan. Bring to a boil. Reduce heat and simmer, covered, 12 minutes or until rice is almost tender. Stir in broccoli, carrots and remaining 2 tablespoons chicken broth. Cook, covered, 2 to 3 minutes more or until vegetables are crisp-tender and rice is tender.

3. Drain chicken; discard marinade. Prepare grill for direct grilling. Grill chicken over medium coals 10 to 13 minutes or until no longer pink in center. Serve chicken with rice mixture. *Makes 2 servings*

Peppery Grilled Salad

1 package (about 1½ pounds) PERDUE® FIT 'N EASY® Fresh Skinless & Boneless Chicken Thighs
1 teaspoon coarsely ground or cracked pepper
3 tablespoons Worcestershire sauce, divided
6 tablespoons olive oil, divided
Salt
1 tablespoon Dijon mustard
2 tablespoons wine vinegar
1 tablespoon minced shallots
1 small head bibb or Boston lettuce, torn into pieces
1 bunch arugula, well rinsed, torn into pieces
1 head Belgian endive, torn into pieces
½ pound green beans, cooked tender-crisp
1 cup cherry tomatoes
1 tablespoon minced fresh basil
1 tablespoon minced parsley

Open thighs and pound to flatten to even thickness. Press pepper into both sides of chicken and place in a shallow baking dish. Add 2 tablespoons Worcestershire sauce; turn chicken to coat well. Cover and refrigerate 1 hour or longer.

Prepare grill for cooking. Brush chicken with 1 tablespoon oil and sprinkle lightly with salt. Grill thighs, uncovered, 5 to 6 inches over medium-hot coals 25 to 30 minutes or until chicken is cooked through, turning occasionally.

In salad bowl, combine remaining Worcestershire, mustard, vinegar and shallots. Gradually whisk in remaining oil. Slice warm thighs and add any meat juices to dressing. Arrange greens around edges of 4 dinner plates. Toss chicken, beans and tomatoes with dressing and mound equal portions in middle of greens. To serve, drizzle salads with any remaining dressing and sprinkle with minced herbs. *Makes 4 servings*

Chicken and Fruit Kabobs

1¾ cups honey
¾ cup fresh lemon juice
½ cup Dijon-style mustard
⅓ cup chopped fresh ginger
4 pounds boneless skinless chicken breasts, cut up
6 fresh plums, pitted and quartered
3 firm bananas, cut into chunks
4 cups fresh pineapple chunks (about half of medium pineapple)

Combine honey, lemon juice, mustard and ginger in small bowl; mix well. Thread chicken and fruit onto skewers, alternating chicken with fruit; brush generously with honey mixture. Place kabobs on grill about 4 inches from heat. Grill 5 minutes on each side, brushing frequently with honey mixture. Grill 10 minutes or until chicken is no longer pink in center, turning and brushing frequently with remaining honey mixture.

Makes 12 servings

Southwest Chicken

2 tablespoons olive oil
1 clove garlic, pressed
1 teaspoon chili powder
1 teaspoon ground cumin
1 teaspoon dried oregano leaves
½ teaspoon salt
1 pound skinless boneless chicken breast halves or thighs

Combine oil, garlic, chili powder, cumin, oregano and salt; brush over both sides of chicken to coat. Grill chicken over medium-hot KINGSFORD® Briquets 8 to 10 minutes or until chicken is no longer pink, turning once. Serve immediately or use in Build a Burrito, Taco Salad or other favorite recipes.

Makes 4 servings

Note: Southwest Chicken can be grilled ahead and refrigerated for several days or frozen for longer storage.

Build a Burrito: Top warm large flour tortillas with strips of Southwest Chicken and your choice of drained canned black beans, cooked brown or white rice, shredded cheese, salsa verde, shredded lettuce, sliced black olives and chopped cilantro. Fold in sides and roll to enclose filling. Heat in microwave oven at HIGH until heated through. (Or, wrap in foil and heat in preheated 350°F oven.)

Taco Salad: For a quick one-dish meal, layer strips of Southwest Chicken with tomato wedges, blue or traditional corn tortilla chips, sliced black olives, shredded romaine or iceberg lettuce, shredded cheese and avocado slices. Serve with salsa, sour cream, guacamole or a favorite dressing.

Grilled Greek Chicken

1 cup MIRACLE WHIP® Salad Dressing
½ cup chopped fresh parsley
¼ cup dry white wine or chicken broth
1 lemon, sliced and halved
2 tablespoons dried oregano leaves, crushed
1 tablespoon garlic powder
1 tablespoon black pepper
2 (2½- to 3-pound) broiler-fryers, cut up

• Mix together all ingredients except chicken until well blended. Pour over chicken. Cover; marinate in refrigerator at least 20 minutes. Drain marinade; discard.

• Place chicken on grill over medium-hot coals (coals will have slight glow). Grill, covered, 20 to 25 minutes on each side or until tender.

Makes 8 servings

Southwest Chicken

Chicken Shish-Kebabs

¼ cup CRISCO® Oil*
¼ cup wine vinegar
¼ cup lemon juice
1 teaspoon dried oregano leaves
1 clove garlic, minced
¼ teaspoon black pepper
1½ pounds boneless, skinless
    chicken breasts, cut into 1- to
    1½-inch cubes
12 bamboo or metal skewers
    (10 to 12 inches long)
2 medium tomatoes, cut into
    wedges
2 medium onions, cut into
    wedges
1 medium green bell pepper, cut
    into 1-inch squares
1 medium red bell pepper, cut
    into 1-inch squares
4 cups hot cooked brown rice
    (cooked without salt or fat)
Salt (optional)

Use your favorite Crisco Oil product.

1. Combine oil, vinegar, lemon juice, oregano, garlic and black pepper in shallow baking dish or glass bowl. Stir well. Add chicken. Stir to coat. Cover. Marinate in refrigerator 3 hours, turning chicken several times.

2. Soak bamboo skewers in water. Heat broiler or prepare grill. Thread chicken, tomatoes, onions and bell peppers alternately on skewers.

3. Place skewers on broiler pan or grill. Broil or grill 5 minutes. Turn. Broil or grill 5 to 7 minutes or to desired doneness. Serve over hot rice. Season with salt and garnish, if desired.

Makes 6 servings

Crunchy Apple Salsa with Grilled Chicken

2 cups Washington Gala apples,
    halved, cored and chopped
¾ cup (1 large) Anaheim chili
    pepper, seeded and
    chopped
½ cup chopped onion
¼ cup lime juice
    Salt and black pepper to taste
    Grilled Chicken (recipe
    follows)

Combine all ingredients except chicken and mix well; set aside to allow flavors to blend about 45 minutes. Prepare Grilled Chicken. Serve salsa over or alongside Grilled Chicken.　　*Makes 3 cups salsa*

Grilled Chicken: Marinate 2 whole boneless, skinless chicken breasts in a mixture of ¼ cup dry white wine, ¼ cup apple juice, ½ teaspoon grated lime peel, ½ teaspoon salt and dash pepper for 20 to 30 minutes. Drain and grill over medium-hot coals, turning once, until chicken is no longer pink in center.

Favorite recipe from **Washington Apple Commission**

Crunchy Apple Salsa with Grilled Chicken

Family Barbecued Chicken

5 pounds chicken pieces
1 cup salad oil
⅓ cup tarragon vinegar
¼ cup sugar
¼ cup ketchup
1 tablespoon Worcestershire sauce
1½ teaspoons dry mustard
1 teaspoon LAWRY'S® Red Pepper Seasoned Salt
1 teaspoon LAWRY'S® Garlic Powder with Parsley

In large resealable plastic food storage bag, combine all ingredients except chicken; mix well. Remove ½ cup marinade for basting. Add chicken; seal bag. Marinate in refrigerator at least 30 minutes. Remove chicken; discard used marinade. To partially cook chicken, place in 13×9-inch baking dish. Bake in 350°F oven 45 minutes. Then, grill or broil chicken 15 to 25 minutes depending on size of piece, turning once and basting often with additional ½ cup marinade. Chicken is done when no longer pink in center and juices run clear when cut. *Do not baste during last 5 minutes of cooking.* Discard any remaining marinade.

Makes 6 servings

Serving Suggestion: Serve with baked beans and a fresh vegetable salad.

Santa Fe Grilled Chicken

Juice of 2 to 3 fresh limes (½ cup), divided
2 tablespoons vegetable oil, divided
1 package (about 3 pounds) PERDUE® Fresh Skinless Pick of the Chicken
Salt and black pepper to taste
1 cup fresh or frozen diced peaches
¼ cup finely chopped red onion
1 jalapeño pepper, seeded and minced
2 cloves garlic, minced
1 teaspoon ground cumin
Chili powder

In medium-sized bowl, combine 7 tablespoons lime juice and 1 tablespoon plus 1½ teaspoons oil. Add chicken, salt and pepper; cover and marinate in the refrigerator 2 to 4 hours. Meanwhile to prepare salsa, in small bowl, combine remaining 1 tablespoon lime juice and 1½ teaspoons oil, peaches, onion, jalapeño pepper, garlic and cumin.

Prepare outdoor grill or preheat broiler. Remove chicken from marinade. Sprinkle with chili powder and place on cooking surface of grill over medium-hot coals or on broiler pan. Grill or broil 6 to 8 inches from heat source, allowing 20 to 30 minutes for breasts and 30 to 40 minutes for thighs and drumsticks, turning occasionally. Serve grilled chicken with salsa. *Makes 4 to 5 servings*

Classic Grilled Chicken

1 whole frying chicken*
   (3½ pounds), quartered
¼ cup lemon juice
¼ cup olive oil
2 tablespoons soy sauce
2 large cloves garlic, minced
½ teaspoon sugar
½ teaspoon ground cumin
¼ teaspoon black pepper

*Substitute 3½ pounds chicken parts for whole chicken, if desired. Grill legs and thighs about 35 minutes and breast halves about 25 minutes or until chicken is no longer pink in center, turning once.

Rinse chicken under cold running water; pat dry with paper towels.

Arrange chicken in 13×9×2-inch glass baking dish. Combine remaining ingredients in small bowl; pour half of mixture over chicken. Cover and refrigerate chicken at least 1 hour or overnight. Cover and reserve remaining mixture in refrigerator to use for basting. Remove chicken from marinade; discard marinade. Arrange medium KINGSFORD® Briquets on each side of large rectangular metal or foil drip pan. Pour hot tap water into drip pan until half full. Place chicken on grid directly above drip pan. Grill chicken, skin side down, on covered grill 25 minutes. Baste with reserved baste. Turn chicken; cook 20 to 25 minutes or until juices run clear and chicken is no longer pink in center.   *Makes 6 servings*

Classic Grilled Chicken

77

Grilled Chicken and Vegetable Kabobs

⅓ cup olive oil
¼ cup lemon juice
4 cloves garlic, coarsely
    chopped
½ teaspoon salt
½ teaspoon lemon pepper
½ teaspoon dried tarragon
    leaves
1 pound chicken tenders
6 ounces mushrooms
1 cup sliced zucchini
½ cup cubed green bell pepper
½ cup cubed red bell pepper
1 red onion, quartered
6 cherry tomatoes
3 cups hot cooked rice

Combine oil, lemon juice, garlic, salt, lemon pepper and tarragon in large resealable plastic food storage bag. Add chicken, mushrooms, zucchini, bell peppers, onion and tomatoes. Seal and shake until well coated. Refrigerate at least 8 hours, turning occasionally.

Soak 6 (10-inch) wooden skewers in water 30 minutes; set aside.

Remove chicken and vegetables from marinade; discard marinade. Thread chicken and vegetables onto skewers.

Coat grill grid with nonstick cooking spray; place skewers on grid. Grill covered over medium-hot coals 3 to 4 minutes on each side or until chicken is no longer pink in center.

Remove chicken and vegetables from skewers and serve over rice.

Makes 6 servings

Serving Suggestion: Serve with sliced fresh pineapple and green grapes.

Grilled Vegetable and Chicken Pasta

Prep and Cook Time: 16 minutes

8 ounces (4 cups) uncooked
    bow-tie pasta
2 red or green bell peppers,
    seeded and cut into quarters
1 medium zucchini, cut into
    halves
3 boneless skinless chicken
    breast halves (about
    1 pound)
½ cup Italian dressing
½ cup prepared pesto sauce

1. Cook pasta according to package directions; drain. Place in large bowl; cover to keep warm.

2. While pasta is cooking, combine vegetables, chicken and dressing in medium bowl; toss well. Grill or broil 6 to 8 minutes on each side or until vegetables are crisp-tender and chicken is no longer pink in center. (Vegetables may take less time than chicken.)

3. Cut vegetables and chicken into bite-size pieces. Add vegetables, chicken and pesto to pasta; toss well.

Makes 4 to 6 servings

Grilled Chicken and Vegetable Kabobs

Grilled Chicken Croissant with Roasted Pepper Dressing

Prep Time: *15 minutes*
Cook Time: *15 minutes*

½ cup *French's*® Dijon Mustard
3 tablespoons olive oil
3 tablespoons red wine vinegar
¾ teaspoon dried Italian
    seasoning
¾ teaspoon garlic powder
1 jar (7 ounces) roasted red
    peppers, drained
1 pound boneless skinless
    chicken breast halves
    Lettuce leaves
4 croissants, split

Whisk together mustard, oil, vinegar, Italian seasoning and garlic powder in small bowl until well blended. Pour ¼ cup mixture into blender. Add peppers. Cover and process until mixture is smooth; set aside.

Brush chicken pieces with remaining mustard mixture. Place pieces on grid. Grill over hot coals 15 minutes or until chicken is no longer pink in center, turning often. To serve, place lettuce leaves on bottom halves of croissants. Arrange chicken on top of lettuce. Spoon roasted pepper dressing over chicken. Cover with croissant top. Garnish as desired.

Makes 4 servings

San Francisco Grilled Chicken

2 boneless, skinless chicken
    breast halves
3 tablespoons Italian or Ranch
    salad dressing
2 slices SARGENTO® Deli Style
    Sliced Muenster or Swiss
    Cheese
2 kaiser rolls, split, *or* 4 slices
    sourdough bread
8 spinach leaves
½ cup alfalfa sprouts
6 avocado slices
2 tablespoons thick salsa

Pound chicken breast halves to ¼-inch thickness. Place in shallow bowl; pour dressing over chicken. Cover; marinate in refrigerator 1 hour. Drain chicken. Grill 3 minutes; turn. Top each chicken breast half with Muenster cheese slice; continue to grill 2 to 3 minutes or until chicken is no longer pink in center. On bottom half of each roll, layer half the spinach leaves, sprouts and avocado slices. Top each sandwich with grilled chicken breast, half of salsa and top half of roll. *Makes 2 sandwiches*

CONTENTS

ENCHANTING CLASSICS

82

HOCUS-POCUS CASSEROLES

96

MAGICAL SKILLET DISHES

114

PRESTO SOUPS, STEWS & CHILI

128

IN A FLASH

144

ENCHANTING CLASSICS

★★★

PIZZA MEAT LOAF

   1 envelope LIPTON® RECIPE SECRETS® Onion Soup Mix*
   2 pounds ground beef
1½ cups fresh bread crumbs
   2 eggs
   1 small green bell pepper, chopped (optional)
¼ cup water
   1 cup RAGÚ® OLD WORLD STYLE® Pasta Sauce
   1 cup shredded mozzarella cheese (about 4 ounces)

Also terrific with LIPTON® RECIPE SECRETS® Savory Herb with Garlic Soup Mix.

1. Preheat oven to 350°F. In large bowl, combine all ingredients except ½ cup pasta sauce and ½ cup cheese.

2. In 13×9-inch baking or roasting pan, shape into loaf. Top with remaining ½ cup pasta sauce.

3. Bake uncovered 50 minutes.

4. Sprinkle top with remaining ½ cup cheese. Bake an additional 10 minutes or until done. Let stand 10 minutes before serving.   *Makes 8 servings*

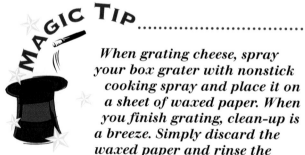

MAGIC TIP

When grating cheese, spray your box grater with nonstick cooking spray and place it on a sheet of waxed paper. When you finish grating, clean-up is a breeze. Simply discard the waxed paper and rinse the grater clean.

DEEP DISH ALL-AMERICAN PIZZA

SAUCE
- 1 pound lean ground beef
- ½ cup chopped onion
- ½ cup chopped green pepper
- 1 cup ketchup
- 1 tablespoon Worcestershire sauce
- 1 teaspoon dry mustard
- 1 teaspoon garlic salt
- ¼ teaspoon black pepper

CRUST
- 3 to 3½ cups all-purpose flour, divided
- 1 package RED STAR® Active Dry Yeast or QUICK•RISE™ Yeast
- 1½ teaspoons salt
- 1 cup warm water
- 3 tablespoons oil

TOPPINGS
- 2 medium firm, ripe tomatoes, sliced
- 1 cup sliced fresh mushrooms
- 2 cups (8 ounces) shredded Cheddar cheese

Preheat oven to 425°F.

Cook and stir beef, onion and green pepper in skillet until meat is lightly browned; drain if necessary. Add ketchup, Worcestershire sauce, mustard, garlic salt and black pepper. Simmer 15 minutes.

In large mixer bowl, combine 1½ cups flour, yeast and salt; mix well. Add very warm water (120° to 130°F) and oil to flour mixture. Blend at low speed until moistened; beat 3 minutes at medium speed. Gradually stir in enough remaining flour to make a firm dough. Knead 3 to 5 minutes on floured surface and roll dough into 16-inch circle or 15×11-inch rectangle. Place in greased 14-inch round deep-dish pizza pan or 13×9-inch baking pan, pushing dough halfway up sides of pan. Cover; let rise in warm place about 15 minutes.

Spread sauce over dough. Arrange tomatoes on sauce. Sprinkle mushrooms on top. Sprinkle with cheese. Bake 20 to 25 minutes or until edge is crisp and golden brown and cheese is melted. Serve immediately.

Makes one 14-inch round or 13×9-inch deep-dish pizza

Tip: Pizza may also be baked in a lasagna pan.

EASY MOSTACCIOLI CASSEROLE

- 1 pound ground beef
- ½ onion, chopped
- 1 can (14½ ounces) tomatoes, chopped and undrained
- 1 can (8 ounces) tomato sauce
- 1 cup chopped olives
- ¼ cup Parmesan cheese
- 2 teaspoons LAWRY'S® Garlic Pepper
- ¼ teaspoons LAWRY'S® Seasoned Salt
- ½ teaspoon oregano
- 8 ounces Mostaccioli noodles, cooked and drained
- 1 cup (8 ounces) grated Mozzarella cheese

In large skillet, brown ground beef until crumbly; drain fat. Add onion, tomatoes, tomato sauce, olives, Parmesan cheese, Garlic Pepper, Seasoned Salt and oregano. Bring to a boil over medium-high heat; reduce heat to low and simmer, uncovered, 20 minutes. In 2-quart ovenproof casserole dish, place hot pasta, cover with meat mixture and top with cheese. Heat under broiler 3 minutes. *Makes 8 servings*

Serving Suggestion: Serve with tossed green salad and herbed French bread.

SPECIAL OCCASION MEAT LOAF

1 pound ground beef
1 pound Italian sausage, removed from casings and crumbled
1½ cups seasoned bread crumbs
2 eggs, lightly beaten
2 tablespoons chopped fresh parsley
2 cloves garlic, minced
1 teaspoon salt
½ teaspoon black pepper
2 cups water
1 tablespoon butter
1 package (about 4 ounces) Spanish rice mix
2 packages (10 ounces each) frozen chopped spinach, thawed and well drained

Combine ground beef, sausage, bread crumbs, eggs, parsley, garlic, salt and pepper in large bowl; mix well. Place on 12×12-inch sheet of aluminum foil moistened with water. Cover with 12×14-inch sheet of waxed paper moistened with water. With hands or rolling pin, press meat mixture into 12×12-inch rectangle. Refrigerate 2 hours or until well chilled.

Bring water, butter and rice mix to a boil in medium saucepan. Continue boiling over medium heat 10 minutes or until rice is tender, stirring occasionally. Refrigerate 2 hours or until well chilled.

Preheat oven to 350°F. Remove waxed paper from ground beef mixture. Spread spinach over ground beef mixture, leaving 1-inch border. Spread rice evenly over spinach. Starting at long end, roll up jelly-roll style, using foil as a guide and removing foil after rolling. Seal edges tightly. Place meat loaf seam-side down in 13×9-inch baking pan. Bake, uncovered, about 1 hour. Let stand 15 minutes before serving. Cut into 1-inch slices.

Makes about 8 servings

MANICOTTI PARMIGIANA

1 package (1.5 ounces) LAWRY'S® Original Style Spaghetti Sauce Spices & Seasonings
1 can (1 pound 12 ounces) whole tomatoes, cut up
1 can (8 ounces) tomato sauce
2 tablespoons LAWRY'S® Garlic Spread Concentrate
12 manicotti shells
1 pound ground beef
¼ cup chopped green bell pepper
½ pound mozzarella cheese, grated
  Grated Parmesan cheese
  Finely chopped parsley (garnish)

In large saucepan, combine the first 4 ingredients. Bring to a boil over medium-high heat; reduce heat to low, cover and simmer 20 minutes, stirring occasionally. Meanwhile, cook manicotti shells according to package directions (about 7 minutes); drain. In medium skillet, brown ground beef and green pepper until beef is crumbly; drain fat. Remove from heat and add mozzarella cheese. Stuff manicotti shells with meat-cheese mixture. Pour ¾ of spaghetti sauce mixture into the bottom of 13×9×2-inch baking dish. Place stuffed manicotti shells over sauce mixture; top with remaining sauce. Sprinkle with Parmesan cheese. Bake, uncovered, in 375°F. oven 30 minutes. *Makes about 8 servings*

Serving Suggestion: Garnish with chopped parsley.

POLYNESIAN BURGERS

¼ cup LAWRY'S® Teriyaki Marinade with
    Pineapple Juice
1 pound ground beef
½ cup chopped green bell pepper
4 onion-flavored hamburger buns
1 can (5¼ ounces) pineapple slices,
    drained
    Lettuce leaves

In medium bowl, combine Teriyaki Marinade, ground beef and bell pepper; mix well. Let stand 10 to 15 minutes. Shape into 4 patties. Grill or broil burgers 8 to 10 minutes or until desired doneness, turning halfway through grilling time. Serve burgers on onion buns topped with pineapple slices and lettuce.

Makes 4 servings

Serving Suggestion: Serve with assorted fresh fruits.

Hint: For extra teriyaki flavor, brush buns and pineapple slices with additional Teriyaki Marinade; grill or broil until buns are lightly toasted and pineapple is heated through.

SLOPPY ONION JOES

1½ pounds ground beef
1 envelope LIPTON® RECIPE SECRETS®
    Onion Soup Mix
1 cup water
1 cup ketchup
2 tablespoons firmly packed brown sugar

1. In 10-inch skillet, brown ground beef over medium-high heat; drain.

2. Stir in remaining ingredients. Bring to a boil over high heat.

3. Reduce heat to low and simmer uncovered, stirring occasionally, 8 minutes or until mixture thickens. Serve, if desired, on hoagie rolls or hamburger buns.

Makes 6 servings

MAGIC TIP

For easy microwave browning of ground beef, place 1 pound of beef in a microwavable colander and set in a deep microwavable bowl. Heat at HIGH 4 to 5 minutes or until the meat is no longer pink, stirring twice during cooking. Discard the grease which accumulates in the bowl.

Polynesian Burger

SOUTHWESTERN MEAT LOAF

1 envelope LIPTON® RECIPE SECRETS®
    Onion Soup Mix*
2 pounds ground beef
2 cups (about 3 ounces) cornflakes or bran
    flakes cereal, crushed
1½ cups frozen or drained canned whole
    kernel corn
1 small green bell pepper, chopped
2 eggs
¾ cup water
⅓ cup ketchup

*Also terrific with LIPTON® RECIPE SECRETS® Onion-
Mushroom or Beefy Onion Soup Mix.*

1. Preheat oven to 350°F. In large bowl,
combine all ingredients.

2. In 13×9-inch baking or roasting pan, shape
into loaf.

3. Bake uncovered 1 hour or until done. Let
stand 10 minutes before serving. Serve, if
desired, with salsa.   *Makes 8 servings*

MAGIC TIP

*For a great lunchbox treat,
wrap leftover meat loaf slices
in a tortilla and top with
your favorite taco toppings
such as salsa, sour cream,
grated cheese and shredded
lettuce.*

MEDITERRANEAN BURGERS

½ cup feta cheese (2 ounces)
¼ cup A.1.® Original or A.1.® BOLD
    & SPICY Steak Sauce, divided
2 tablespoons sliced pitted ripe olives
2 tablespoons mayonnaise
1 pound ground beef
4 (5-inch) pita breads
4 radicchio leaves
4 tomato slices

Mix feta cheese, 2 tablespoons steak sauce,
olives and mayonnaise. Cover; refrigerate at
least one hour or up to 2 days.

Shape beef into 4 patties. Grill burgers over
medium heat or broil 6 inches from heat source
5 minutes on each side or until no longer pink
in center, basting with remaining 2 tablespoons
steak sauce.

Split open top edge of each pita bread. Arrange
1 radicchio leaf in each pita pocket; top each
with burger, tomato slice and 2 tablespoons
chilled sauce. Serve immediately.

Makes 4 servings

SAUCY STUFFED PEPPERS

6 medium green bell peppers
1¼ cups water
2 cups low-sodium tomato juice, divided
1 can (6 ounces) tomato paste
1 teaspoon dried oregano leaves, crushed, divided
½ teaspoon dried basil leaves, crushed
½ teaspoon garlic powder, divided
1 pound lean ground beef
1½ cups QUAKER® Oats (quick or old fashioned, uncooked)
1 medium tomato, chopped
¼ cup chopped carrot
¼ cup chopped onion

Heat oven to 350°F. Cut peppers in half lengthwise. Remove membranes and seeds; set peppers aside. In large saucepan, combine water, 1 cup tomato juice, tomato paste, ½ teaspoon oregano, basil and ¼ teaspoon garlic powder. Simmer 10 to 15 minutes.

Combine beef, oats, remaining 1 cup tomato juice, ½ teaspoon oregano and ¼ teaspoon garlic powder with tomato, carrot and onion; mix well. Fill each pepper half with about ⅓ cup meat mixture. Place in 13×9-inch glass baking dish; pour sauce evenly over peppers. Bake 45 to 50 minutes.   *Makes 12 servings*

TEMPTING TACO BURGERS

1 envelope LIPTON® RECIPE SECRETS® Onion-Mushroom Soup Mix*
1 pound ground beef
½ cup chopped tomato
¼ cup finely chopped green bell pepper
1 teaspoon chili powder
¼ cup water

*Also terrific with LIPTON® RECIPE SECRETS® Onion, Garlic Mushroom, Beefy Onion or Beefy Mushroom Soup Mix.

1. In large bowl, combine all ingredients; shape into 4 patties.

2. Grill or broil until done. Serve, if desired, on hamburger buns and top with shredded lettuce and Cheddar cheese.   *Makes 4 servings*

Recipe Tip: The best way to test for doneness of beef, pork, fish and poultry is to use a meat thermometer or an instant read thermometer, inserted into the thickest part of the meat.

MINI MEAT LOAVES & VEGETABLES

1½ pounds lean ground beef
 1 egg
 1 can (8 ounces) tomato sauce, divided
1⅓ cups *French's® Taste Toppers™* French
    Fried Onions, divided
 ½ teaspoon salt
 ½ teaspoon Italian seasoning
 6 small red potatoes, thinly sliced (about
    1½ cups)
 1 bag (16 ounces) frozen vegetable
    combination (broccoli, corn, red
    pepper), thawed and drained
   Salt
   Black pepper

Preheat oven to 375°F. In medium bowl, combine ground beef, egg, ½ *can* tomato sauce, ⅔ cup **Taste Toppers**, ½ teaspoon salt and Italian seasoning. Shape into 3 mini loaves and place in 13×9-inch baking dish. Arrange potatoes around loaves. Bake, covered, at 375°F for 35 minutes. Spoon vegetables around meat loaves; stir to combine with potatoes. Lightly season vegetables with salt and pepper, if desired. Top meat loaves with remaining tomato sauce. Bake, uncovered, 15 minutes or until meat loaves are done. Top loaves with remaining ⅔ cup **Taste Toppers**; bake, uncovered, 3 minutes or until **Taste Toppers** are golden brown.   *Makes 6 servings*

Microwave Directions: Prepare meat loaves as directed above. Arrange potatoes on bottom of 12×8-inch microwave-safe dish; place meat loaves on potatoes. Cook, covered, on HIGH 13 minutes. Rotate dish halfway through cooking time. Add vegetables and season as above. Top meat loaves with remaining tomato sauce. Cook, covered, 7 minutes or until meat loaves are done. Rotate dish halfway through cooking time. Top loaves with remaining ⅔ cup onions; cook, uncovered, 1 minute. Let stand 5 minutes.

LIPTON® ONION BURGERS

2 pounds ground beef
1 envelope LIPTON® RECIPE SECRETS®
   Onion Soup Mix*
½ cup water

*Also terrific with LIPTON® RECIPE SECRETS® Beefy Onion, Onion-Mushroom, Beefy Mushroom or Savory Herb with Garlic, or Garlic Mushroom Soup Mix.

1. In large bowl, combine all ingredients; shape into 8 patties.

2. Grill or broil to desired doneness.
                    Makes about 8 servings

MAGIC TIP

Use the direct cooking method for quick-cooking foods such as hamburgers. For this method, arrange the coals in a single layer directly under the food.

LASAGNA SUPREME

8 ounces lasagna noodles
½ pound ground beef
½ pound mild Italian sausage, casings removed
1 medium onion, chopped
2 cloves garlic, minced
1 can (14½ ounces) whole peeled tomatoes, undrained and chopped
1 can (6 ounces) tomato paste
2 teaspoons dried basil leaves
1 teaspoon dried marjoram leaves
1 can (4 ounces) sliced mushrooms, drained
2 eggs
1 pound cream-style cottage cheese
¾ cup grated Parmesan cheese, divided
2 tablespoons dried parsley flakes
½ teaspoon salt
½ teaspoon black pepper
2 cups (8 ounces) shredded Cheddar cheese
3 cups (12 ounces) shredded mozzarella cheese

1. Cook lasagna noodles according to package directions; drain.

2. Cook meats, onion and garlic in large skillet over medium-high heat until meat is brown, stirring to separate meat. Drain.

3. Add tomatoes with juice, tomato paste, basil and marjoram. Reduce heat to low. Cover; simmer 15 minutes, stirring often. Stir in mushrooms; set aside.

4. Preheat oven to 375°F. Beat eggs in large bowl; add cottage cheese, ½ cup Parmesan cheese, parsley, salt and pepper. Mix well.

5. Place half the noodles into the bottom of 13×9-inch baking pan. Spread half the cottage cheese mixture over noodles, then half the meat mixture and half the Cheddar cheese and mozzarella cheese. Repeat layers. Sprinkle with remaining ¼ cup Parmesan cheese.

6. Bake lasagna 40 to 45 minutes or until bubbly. Let stand 10 minutes before cutting.

Makes 8 to 10 servings

Note: Lasagna may be assembled, covered and refrigerated up to 2 days in advance. Bake, uncovered, in preheated 375°F oven 60 minutes or until bubbly.

MAGIC TIP

Store ground meat in the coldest part of the refrigerator (40°F) for up to 2 days. Be sure to always cook ground meat until it is browned, to a minimum of 155°F.

Lasagna Supreme

GRILLED MEAT LOAVES AND POTATOES

1 pound ground beef
½ cup A.1.® Original or A.1.® BOLD
   & SPICY Steak Sauce, divided
½ cup plain dry bread crumbs
1 egg, beaten
¼ cup finely chopped green bell pepper
¼ cup finely chopped onion
2 tablespoons margarine or butter, melted
4 (6-ounce) red skin potatoes, blanched,
   sliced into ¼-inch-thick rounds
   Grated Parmesan cheese
   Additional A.1.® Original or A.1.® BOLD
   & SPICY Steak Sauce (optional)

Mix ground beef, ¼ cup steak sauce, bread crumbs, egg, pepper and onion. Shape mixture into 4 (4-inch) oval-shaped loaves; set aside.

Blend remaining ¼ cup steak sauce and margarine; set aside.

Grill meat loaves over medium heat 20 to 25 minutes and potato slices 10 to 12 minutes or until beef is no longer pink in center and potatoes are tender, turning and basting both occasionally with reserved steak sauce mixture. Sprinkle cheese on potatoes. Serve immediately with additional steak sauce if desired.

Makes 4 servings

LASAGNA ROLL-UPS

1 pound ground beef
1 (16-ounce) jar spaghetti sauce
¼ cup A.1.® Steak Sauce
½ teaspoon dried basil leaves
1 (15-ounce) container ricotta cheese
1 egg, beaten
¼ cup grated Parmesan cheese, divided
8 lasagna noodles, cooked
2 cups shredded mozzarella cheese
   (8 ounces)

Brown ground beef in skillet over medium-high heat, stirring occasionally to break up meat; drain. In small bowl, mix spaghetti sauce, steak sauce and basil; stir half the sauce mixture into beef. In another bowl, mix ricotta cheese, egg and 2 tablespoons Parmesan cheese.

On each lasagna noodle, spread about ¼ cup ricotta mixture. Top with about ⅓ cup beef mixture and ¼ cup mozzarella cheese. Roll up each noodle from short end; stand on end in greased 2-quart casserole. Pour remaining sauce over noodles. Sprinkle with remaining Parmesan cheese.

Bake at 350°F for 45 minutes or until hot and bubbly. Serve with additional Parmesan cheese if desired. *Makes 4 to 6 servings*

Microwave Directions: In 2-quart microwave-safe casserole, crumble beef; cover. Microwave at HIGH (100% power) for 5 to 6 minutes or until browned; drain. Mix spaghetti sauce, steak sauce and basil; stir half the sauce mixture into beef. Fill lasagna rolls as above; arrange in same 2-quart casserole. Top with remaining sauce and parmesan cheese; cover. Microwave at HIGH for 10 to 12 minutes or until hot and bubbly, rotating dish ½ turn after 5 minutes. Let stand 3 minutes before serving.

Grilled Meat Loaf and Potatoes

HOCUS-POCUS CASSEROLES

★★★

BEEFY NACHO CRESCENT BAKE

 1 pound lean ground beef
½ cup chopped onion
¼ teaspoon salt
⅛ teaspoon black pepper
 1 tablespoon chili powder
 1 teaspoon ground cumin
 1 teaspoon dried oregano leaves
 1 can (11 ounces) condensed nacho cheese soup, undiluted
 1 cup milk
 1 can (8 ounces) refrigerated crescent roll dough
¼ cup (1 ounce) shredded Cheddar cheese
   Chopped fresh cilantro (optional)
   Salsa (optional)

Preheat oven to 375°F. Spray 13×9-inch baking dish with nonstick cooking spray. Place beef and onion in large skillet; season with salt and pepper. Brown beef over medium-high heat until no longer pink, stirring to separate meat. Drain fat. Stir in chili powder, cumin and oregano. Cook and stir 2 minutes; remove from heat.

Combine soup and milk in medium bowl, stirring until smooth. Pour soup mixture into prepared dish, spreading evenly.

Separate crescent dough into 4 rectangles; press perforations together firmly. Roll each rectangle to 8×4 inches. (Sprinkle with flour to minimize sticking, if necessary.) Cut each rectangle in half crosswise to form 8 (4-inch) squares.

Spoon about ¼ cup beef mixture into center of each square. Lift 4 corners of dough up over filling to meet in center; pinch and twist firmly to seal. Place squares in dish.

Bake, uncovered, 20 to 25 minutes or until crusts are golden brown. Sprinkle cheese over squares. Bake 5 minutes or until cheese melts. To serve, spoon soup mixture in dish over each serving; sprinkle with cilantro, if desired. Serve with salsa, if desired. *Makes 4 servings*

BEEF STROGANOFF CASSEROLE

1 pound lean ground beef
¼ teaspoon salt
⅛ teaspoon black pepper
1 teaspoon vegetable oil
8 ounces sliced mushrooms
1 large onion, chopped
3 cloves garlic, minced
¼ cup dry white wine
1 can (10¾ ounces) condensed cream
   of mushroom soup, undiluted
½ cup sour cream
1 tablespoon Dijon mustard
4 cups cooked egg noodles
Chopped fresh parsley (optional)

Preheat oven to 350°F. Spray 13×9-inch baking dish with nonstick cooking spray.

Place beef in large skillet; season with salt and pepper. Brown beef over medium-high heat until no longer pink, stirring to separate beef. Drain fat from skillet; set beef aside.

Heat oil in same skillet over medium-high heat until hot. Add mushrooms, onion and garlic; cook 2 minutes or until onion is tender, stirring often. Add wine; reduce heat to medium-low and simmer 3 minutes. Remove from heat; stir in soup, sour cream and mustard until well combined. Return beef to skillet.

Place noodles in prepared dish. Pour beef mixture over noodles; stir until noodles are well coated.

Bake, uncovered, 30 minutes or until heated through. Sprinkle with parsley, if desired.

Makes 6 servings

CALIFORNIA TAMALE PIE

1 pound ground beef
1 cup yellow corn meal
2 cups milk
2 eggs, beaten
1 package (1.48 ounces) LAWRY'S® Spices
   & Seasonings for Chili
2 teaspoons LAWRY'S® Seasoned Salt
1 can (17 ounces) whole kernel corn,
   drained
1 can (14½ ounces) whole tomatoes,
   cut up
1 can (2¼ ounces) sliced ripe olives,
   drained
1 cup (4 ounces) shredded cheddar cheese

In medium skillet, cook ground beef until browned and crumbly; drain fat. In 2½-quart casserole dish, combine corn meal, milk and egg; mix well. Add ground beef and remaining ingredients except cheese; stir to mix. Bake, uncovered, in 350°F oven 1 hour and 15 minutes. Add cheese and continue baking until cheese melts. Let stand 10 minutes before serving.

Microwave Directions: In 2½-quart glass casserole, microwave ground beef on HIGH 5 to 6 minutes; drain fat and crumble beef. Mix in corn meal, milk and egg; blend well. Add remaining ingredients except cheese. Cover with plastic wrap, venting one corner. Microwave on HIGH 15 minutes, stirring after 8 minutes. Sprinkle cheese over top and microwave on HIGH 2 minutes. Let stand 10 minutes before serving.

Makes 6 to 8 servings

Serving Suggestion: Serve with mixed green salad flavored with kiwi and green onion.

Hint: Substitute 1 package (1.25 ounces) LAWRY'S® Taco Spices & Seasonings for Spices & Seasonings for Chili Seasoning Mix, if desired.

Beef Stroganoff Casserole

SPINACH-POTATO BAKE

1 pound extra-lean (90% lean) ground
    beef
½ cup sliced fresh mushrooms
1 small onion, chopped
2 cloves garlic, minced
1 package (10 ounces) frozen chopped
    spinach, thawed, well drained
½ teaspoon ground nutmeg
1 pound russet potatoes, peeled, cooked
    and mashed
¼ cup light sour cream
¼ cup fat-free (skim) milk
    Salt and black pepper
½ cup (2 ounces) shredded Cheddar cheese

Preheat oven to 400°F. Spray deep 9-inch
casserole dish with nonstick cooking spray.

Brown ground beef in large skillet. Drain. Add
mushrooms, onion and garlic; cook until
tender. Stir in spinach and nutmeg; cover. Heat
thoroughly, stirring occasionally.

Combine potatoes, sour cream and milk. Add to
ground beef mixture; season with salt and
pepper to taste. Spoon into prepared casserole
dish; sprinkle with cheese.

Bake 15 to 20 minutes or until slightly puffed
and cheese is melted. *Makes 6 servings*

MAGIC TIP

*USDA standards require that
all ground beef be at least
70 percent lean. Ground
sirloin and ground round are
the leanest. Ground chuck
contains more fat, so it
produces juicier hamburgers
and many other beef dishes.*

MALAYSIAN CURRIED BEEF

2 tablespoons vegetable oil
2 large yellow onions, chopped
1 piece fresh ginger (about 1-inch square),
    minced
2 cloves garlic, minced
2 tablespoons curry powder
1 teaspoon salt
2 large baking potatoes (1 pound), peeled
    and cut into chunks
1 cup beef broth
1 pound ground beef chuck
2 ripe tomatoes (12 ounces), peeled and
    cut into chunks
    Hot cooked rice
    Purple kale and watercress sprigs for
    garnish

1. Heat wok over medium-high heat 1 minute
or until hot. Drizzle oil into wok and heat
30 seconds. Add onions and stir-fry 2 minutes.
Add ginger, garlic, curry and salt to wok. Cook
and stir about 1 minute or until fragrant. Add
potatoes; cook and stir 2 to 3 minutes.

2. Add beef broth to potato mixture. Cover and
bring to a boil. Reduce heat to low; simmer
about 20 minutes or until potatoes are fork-
tender.

3. Stir ground beef into potato mixture. Cook
and stir about 5 minutes or until beef is browned
and no pink remains; spoon off fat, if necessary.

4. Add tomato chunks and stir gently until
thoroughly heated. Spoon beef mixture into
serving dish. Top center with rice. Garnish, if
desired. *Makes 4 servings*

PASTA "PIZZA"

3 eggs, slightly beaten
½ cup milk
2 cups corkscrew macaroni, cooked and
    drained
½ cup (2 ounces) shredded Wisconsin
    Cheddar cheese
¼ cup finely chopped onion
1 pound lean ground beef
1 can (15 ounces) tomato sauce
1 teaspoon dried basil leaves
1 teaspoon dried oregano leaves
½ teaspoon garlic salt
1 medium tomato, thinly sliced
1 green pepper, sliced into rings
1½ cups (6 ounces) shredded Wisconsin
    Mozzarella cheese

Combine eggs and milk in small bowl. Add to hot macaroni; mix lightly to coat. Stir in Cheddar cheese and onion; mix well. Spread macaroni mixture onto bottom of well-buttered 14-inch pizza pan. Bake at 350°F for 25 minutes. Meanwhile, in large skillet over medium-high heat, brown meat, stirring occasionally to separate meat; drain. Stir in tomato sauce, basil, oregano and garlic salt. Spoon over macaroni crust. Arrange tomato slices and pepper rings on top. Sprinkle with Mozzarella cheese. Continue baking 15 minutes or until cheese is bubbly.   *Makes 8 servings*

Prep time: 50 minutes

*Favorite recipe from **Wisconsin Milk Marketing Board***

ZUCCHINI LASAGNE

3 cans (8 ounces each) CONTADINA®
    Tomato Sauce
1 can (14.5 ounces) CONTADINA® Stewed
    Tomatoes, undrained
1 teaspoon granulated sugar
1 teaspoon Italian herb seasoning
1 teaspoon ground black pepper
1 pound lean ground beef
3 teaspoons seasoned salt
6 medium zucchini squash, sliced ⅛ inch
    thick
2 cups (8 ounces) shredded mozzarella
    cheese
2 cups (15 ounces) ricotta cheese
3 tablespoons grated Parmesan cheese

1. Combine tomato sauce, stewed tomatoes, sugar, Italian seasoning and pepper in medium saucepan.

2. Simmer, uncovered, for 25 minutes, stirring occasionally. In medium skillet, brown beef; drain. Stir in seasoned salt and tomato sauce mixture.

3. Butter bottom of 13×9-inch baking dish. Layer half of zucchini slices on bottom of baking dish; sprinkle lightly with salt. Spread half of ground beef mixture over zucchini. Sprinkle with mozzarella cheese and evenly spread all the ricotta cheese. Top with remaining zucchini slices; sprinkle lightly with salt. Spread with remaining beef mixture. Sprinkle Parmesan cheese on top.

4. Bake in preheated 350°F oven for 45 minutes.   *Makes 8 cups*

Prep Time: 20 minutes
Cook Time: 70 minutes

TACOS IN PASTA SHELLS

1 package (3 ounces) cream cheese with chives
18 jumbo pasta shells
1¼ pounds ground beef
1 teaspoon salt
1 teaspoon chili powder
2 tablespoons butter, melted
1 cup prepared taco sauce
1 cup (4 ounces) shredded Cheddar cheese
1 cup (4 ounces) shredded Monterey Jack cheese
1½ cups crushed tortilla chips
1 cup sour cream
3 green onions, chopped
Leaf lettuce, small pitted ripe olives and cherry tomatoes, for garnish

1. Cut cream cheese into ½-inch cubes. Let stand at room temperature until softened.

2. Cook pasta according to package directions. Place in colander and rinse under warm running water. Drain well. Return to saucepan.

3. Preheat oven to 350°F. Butter 13×9-inch baking pan.

4. Cook beef in large skillet over medium-high heat until brown, stirring to separate meat; drain drippings.

5. Reduce heat to medium-low. Add cream cheese, salt and chili powder; simmer 5 minutes.

6. Toss shells with butter. Fill shells with beef mixture. Arrange shells in prepared pan. Pour taco sauce over each shell. Cover with foil.

7. Bake 15 minutes. Uncover; top with Cheddar cheese, Monterey Jack cheese and chips. Bake 15 minutes more or until bubbly. Top with sour cream and onions. Garnish, if desired.

Makes 4 to 6 servings

MAGIC TIP

Keep packages of raw meat away from other food items, especially from produce and unwrapped products. The meat's juices can drip and contaminate other foods.

Tacos in Pasta Shells

SHEPHERD'S PIE

1⅓ cups instant mashed potato buds
1⅔ cups milk
2 tablespoons margarine or butter
1 teaspoon salt, divided
1 pound ground beef
¼ teaspoon black pepper
1 jar (12 ounces) beef gravy
1 package (10 ounces) frozen mixed
    vegetables, thawed and drained
¾ cup grated Parmesan cheese

1. Preheat broiler. Prepare 4 servings of mashed potatoes according to package directions using milk, margarine and ½ teaspoon salt.

2. While mashed potatoes are cooking, brown meat in medium broilerproof skillet over medium-high heat, stirring to separate meat. Drain drippings. Sprinkle meat with remaining ½ teaspoon salt and pepper. Add gravy and vegetables; mix well. Cook over medium-low heat 5 minutes or until hot.

3. Spoon prepared potatoes around outside edge of skillet, leaving 3-inch circle in center. Sprinkle cheese evenly over potatoes. Broil 4 to 5 inches from heat source 3 minutes or until cheese is golden brown and meat mixture is bubbly. *Makes 4 servings*

Prep and Cook Time: 28 minutes

ARTICHOKE CASSEROLE

¾ pound extra-lean (90% lean) ground
    beef
½ cup sliced mushrooms
¼ cup chopped onion
1 clove garlic, minced
1 can (14 ounces) artichoke hearts,
    drained, rinsed, chopped
½ cup dry bread crumbs
¼ cup (1 ounce) grated Parmesan cheese
2 tablespoons chopped fresh rosemary *or*
    1 teaspoon dried rosemary
1½ teaspoons chopped fresh marjoram *or*
    ½ teaspoon dried marjoram leaves
Salt and black pepper
3 egg whites

Preheat oven to 400°F. Spray 1-quart casserole with nonstick cooking spray.

Brown ground beef in medium skillet. Drain. Add mushrooms, onion and garlic; cook until tender.

Combine ground beef mixture, artichokes, crumbs, cheese, rosemary and marjoram; mix lightly. Season with salt and pepper to taste.

Beat egg whites until stiff peaks form; fold into ground beef mixture. Spoon into prepared casserole.

Bake 20 minutes or until lightly browned around edges. *Makes 4 servings*

Shepherd's Pie

STRING PIE

1 pound ground beef
½ cup chopped onion
¼ cup chopped green pepper
1 jar (15½ ounces) spaghetti sauce
8 ounces spaghetti, cooked and drained
⅓ cup grated Parmesan cheese
2 eggs, beaten
2 teaspoons butter
1 cup cottage cheese
½ cup (2 ounces) shredded mozzarella cheese

Preheat oven to 350°F. Cook beef, onion and green pepper in large skillet over medium-high heat until meat is browned. Drain fat. Stir in spaghetti sauce. Combine spaghetti, Parmesan cheese, eggs and butter in large bowl; mix well. Place in bottom of 13×9-inch baking pan. Spread cottage cheese over top; cover with sauce mixture. Sprinkle with mozzarella cheese. Bake until mixture is thoroughly heated and cheese is melted, about 20 minutes.

Makes 6 to 8 servings

Favorite recipe from **North Dakota Beef Commission**

RANCH LENTIL CASSEROLE

2 cups lentils, rinsed
4 cups water
1 pound lean ground beef
1 cup water
1 cup ketchup
1 envelope dry onion soup mix
1 teaspoon prepared mustard
1 teaspoon vinegar

Cook lentils in 4 cups water for 30 minutes. Drain. Brown ground beef. Combine lentils, beef, 1 cup water and remaining ingredients in baking dish. Bake at 400°F for 30 minutes.

Makes 8 servings

Note: Prepared recipe can be frozen.

Favorite recipe from **USA Dry Pea & Lentil Council**

MAGIC TIP

Beef can fit into a healthy meal plan. It provides high-quality protein and is also an important source of dietary iron and zinc.

String Pie

MEXICAN STUFFED SHELLS

1 pound ground beef
1 jar (12 ounces) mild or medium picante sauce
½ cup water
1 can (8 ounces) tomato sauce
1 can (4 ounces) chopped green chilies, drained
1⅓ cups *French's® Taste Toppers™* French Fried Onions
1 cup (4 ounces) shredded Monterey Jack cheese, divided
12 pasta stuffing shells, cooked in unsalted water and drained

Preheat oven to 350°F. In large skillet, brown ground beef; drain. In small bowl, combine picante sauce, water and tomato sauce. Stir ½ cup sauce mixture into beef along with chilies, ½ cup cheese and ⅔ *cup Taste Toppers*; mix well. Spread half the remaining sauce mixture in bottom of 10-inch round baking dish. Stuff cooked shells with beef mixture. Arrange shells in baking dish; top with remaining sauce. Bake, covered, at 350°F for 30 minutes or until heated through. Top with remaining ⅔ *cup Taste Toppers* and cheese; bake, uncovered, 5 minutes or until cheese is melted.

Makes 6 servings

Microwave Directions: Crumble ground beef into medium microwave-safe bowl. Cook, covered, on HIGH (100%) 4 to 6 minutes or until beef is cooked. Stir beef halfway through cooking time. Drain well. Prepare sauce mixture as above; spread ½ cup in 12×8-inch microwave-safe dish. Prepare beef mixture as above. Stuff cooked shells with beef mixture. Arrange shells in dish; top with remaining sauce. Cook, covered, 10 to 12 minutes or until heated through. Rotate dish halfway through cooking time. Top with remaining onions and cheese; cook, uncovered, 1 minute or until cheese is melted. Let stand 5 minutes.

MONTEREY BLACK BEAN TORTILLA SUPPER

1 pound ground beef, browned and drained
1½ cups bottled salsa
1 (15-ounce) can black beans, drained
4 (8-inch) flour tortillas
2 cups (8 ounces) shredded Wisconsin Monterey Jack cheese*

*For authentic Mexican flavor, substitute 2 cups shredded Wisconsin Queso Blanco.

Heat oven to 400°F. Combine ground beef, salsa and beans. In lightly greased 2-quart round casserole, layer one tortilla, ⅔ cup meat mixture and ½ cup cheese. Repeat layers three times. Bake 30 minutes or until heated through.

Makes 5 to 6 servings

*Favorite recipe from **Wisconsin Milk Marketing Board***

STUFFED MEXICAN PIZZA PIE

1 pound ground beef
1 large onion, chopped
1 large green bell pepper, chopped
1½ cups UNCLE BEN'S® Instant Rice
2 cans (14½ ounces each) Mexican-style stewed tomatoes, undrained
⅔ cup water
2 cups (8 ounces) shredded Mexican-style seasoned Monterey Jack-Colby cheese blend, divided
1 container (10 ounces) refrigerated pizza crust dough

1. Preheat oven to 425°F. Spray 13×9-inch baking pan with cooking spray; set aside.

2. Spray large nonstick skillet with nonstick cooking spray; heat over high heat until hot. Add beef, onion and bell pepper; cook and stir 5 minutes or until meat is no longer pink.

3. Add rice, stewed tomatoes and water. Bring to a boil. Pour beef mixture into prepared baking pan. Sprinkle with 1¼ cups cheese and stir until blended.

4. Unroll pizza crust dough on work surface. Place dough in one even layer over mixture in baking pan. Cut 6 to 8 slits in dough with sharp knife. Bake 10 minutes or until crust is lightly browned. Sprinkle top of crust with remaining ¾ cup cheese; continue baking 4 minutes or until cheese is melted and crust is deep golden brown.

5. Let stand 5 minutes before cutting.

Makes 6 servings

BEEF & ZUCCHINI QUICHE

1 unbaked 9-inch pie shell
½ pound lean ground beef
1 medium zucchini, shredded
3 green onions, sliced
¼ cup sliced mushrooms
1 tablespoon all-purpose flour
3 eggs, beaten
1 cup milk
¾ cup (3 ounces) shredded Swiss cheese
1½ teaspoons chopped fresh thyme *or*
    ½ teaspoon dried thyme leaves
½ teaspoon salt
    Dash black pepper
    Dash ground red pepper

Preheat oven to 475°F.

Line pie shell with foil; fill with dried beans or rice. Bake 8 minutes. Remove from oven; carefully remove foil and beans. Return pie shell to oven. Continue baking 4 minutes; set aside. *Reduce oven temperature to 375°F.*

Brown ground beef in medium skillet. Drain. Add zucchini, onions and mushrooms; cook, stirring occasionally, until vegetables are tender. Stir in flour; cook 2 minutes, stirring constantly. Remove from heat.

Combine eggs, milk, cheese and seasonings in medium bowl. Stir into ground beef mixture; pour into crust.

Bake 35 minutes or until knife inserted near center comes out clean. *Makes 6 servings*

TAMALE PIE

1 tablespoon olive or vegetable oil
1 small onion, chopped
1 pound ground beef
1 envelope LIPTON® RECIPE SECRETS®
    Onion Soup Mix*
1 can (14½ ounces) stewed tomatoes,
    undrained
½ cup water
1 can (15 to 19 ounces) red kidney beans,
    rinsed and drained
1 package (8½ ounces) corn muffin mix

Also terrific with LIPTON® RECIPE SECRETS® Fiesta Herb with Red Pepper, Onion-Mushroom, Beefy Onion or Beefy Mushroom Soup Mix.

• Preheat oven to 400°F.

• In 12-inch skillet, heat oil over medium heat and cook onion, stirring occasionally, 3 minutes or until tender. Stir in ground beef and cook until browned.

• Stir in onion soup mix blended with tomatoes and water. Bring to a boil over high heat, stirring with spoon to crush tomatoes. Reduce heat to low and stir in beans. Simmer uncovered, stirring occasionally, 10 minutes. Turn into 2-quart casserole.

• Prepare corn muffin mix according to package directions. Spoon evenly over casserole.

• Bake uncovered 15 minutes or until corn topping is golden and filling is hot.

Makes about 6 servings

GREEK-STYLE LASAGNA

1 pound ground beef
1 cup chopped onion
1 clove garlic, crushed OR ¼ teaspoon
    LAWRY'S® Garlic Powder with Parsley
1 teaspoon LAWRY'S® Seasoned Salt
½ teaspoon LAWRY'S® Seasoned Pepper
1 package (1.5 ounces) LAWRY'S® Original
    Style Spaghetti Sauce Spices
    & Seasonings
1 can (6 ounces) tomato paste
2 cups water
¼ cup flour
½ teaspoon LAWRY'S® Seasoned Salt
1 eggplant
¾ cup salad oil
1 cup grated Parmesan cheese

In large skillet, cook ground beef until browned and crumbly; drain fat. Add onion, garlic, 1 teaspoon Seasoned Salt, Seasoned Pepper, Original Style Spaghetti Sauce Spices & Seasonings, tomato paste and water. Bring to a boil over medium-high heat, reduce heat to low, cover and simmer 15 minutes, stirring occasionally. Meanwhile, in small bowl, combine flour and ½ teaspoon Seasoned Salt. Peel eggplant and slice crosswise into ¼-inch-thick slices. Place small amount of salad oil in medium skillet and heat. Lightly coat eggplant slices with seasoned flour. Quickly cook eggplant slices over medium-high heat, adding oil as necessary. (Use as little oil as possible.) Pour ¼ of meat sauce into a 12×8×2-inch baking dish. Cover meat sauce with ⅓ of eggplant slices. Sprinkle ¼ of Parmesan cheese over eggplant. Repeat layers 2 more times, ending with meat sauce and Parmesan cheese. Bake, uncovered, in 350 F. oven 30 minutes.

Makes 6 to 8 servings

Serving Suggestion: Serve with tossed green salad and fruit dessert.

Tamale Pie

LASAGNA BEEF 'N' SPINACH ROLL-UPS

1½ pounds ground beef
1 (28-ounce) jar spaghetti sauce
½ cup A.1.® Original or A.1.® BOLD
    & SPICY Steak Sauce
½ teaspoon dried basil leaves
1 (15-ounce) container ricotta cheese
1 (10-ounce) package frozen chopped
    spinach, thawed, well drained
2 cups shredded mozzarella cheese
    (8 ounces)
⅓ cup grated Parmesan cheese, divided
1 egg, beaten
12 lasagna noodles, cooked, drained
2 tablespoons chopped fresh parsley

In large skillet, over medium-high heat, brown beef until no longer pink, stirring occasionally to break up beef; drain. In small bowl, mix spaghetti sauce, steak sauce and basil; stir 1 cup spaghetti sauce mixture into beef. Set aside remaining sauce mixture.

In medium bowl, mix ricotta cheese, spinach, mozzarella cheese, 3 tablespoons Parmesan cheese and egg. On each lasagna noodle, spread about ¼ cup ricotta mixture. Top with about ⅓ cup beef mixture. Roll up each noodle from short end; lay each roll, seam side down, in lightly greased 13×9×2-inch baking dish. Pour reserved spaghetti sauce mixture over noodles. Sprinkle with remaining Parmesan cheese and parsley. Bake, covered, at 350°F 30 minutes. Uncover and bake 15 to 20 minutes more or until hot and bubbly. Serve with additional Parmesan cheese if desired. Garnish as desired. *Makes 6 servings*

HEARTLAND SHEPHERD'S PIE

¾ pound ground beef
1 medium onion, chopped
1 can (14½ ounces) DEL MONTE® Original
    Recipe Stewed Tomatoes
1 can (8 ounces) DEL MONTE® Tomato
    Sauce
1 can (14½ ounces) DEL MONTE® Mixed
    Vegetables, drained
    Instant mashed potato flakes plus
    ingredients to prepare (enough for
    6 servings)
3 cloves garlic, minced (optional)

1. Preheat oven to 375°F. In large skillet, brown meat and onion over medium-high heat; drain.

2. Add tomatoes and tomato sauce; cook over high heat until thickened, stirring frequently. Stir in mixed vegetables. Season with salt and pepper, if desired.

3. Spoon into 2-quart baking dish; set aside. Prepare 6 servings mashed potatoes according to package directions, first cooking garlic in specified amount of butter.

4. Top meat mixture with potatoes. Bake 20 minutes or until heated through. Garnish with chopped parsley, if desired.

Makes 4 to 6 servings

Prep Time: 5 minutes
Cook Time: 30 minutes

Lasagna Beef 'n' Spinach Roll-Ups

MAGICAL SKILLET DISHES

★★★

CHUCKWAGON BBQ RICE ROUND-UP

1 pound lean ground beef
1 (6.8-ounce) package RICE-A-RONI® Beef Flavor
2 tablespoons margarine or butter
2 cups frozen corn
½ cup prepared barbecue sauce
½ cup (2 ounces) shredded Cheddar cheese

1. In large skillet over medium-high heat, brown ground beef until well cooked. Remove from skillet; drain. Set aside.

2. In same skillet over medium heat, sauté rice-vermicelli mix with margarine until vermicelli is golden brown.

3. Slowly stir in 2½ cups water, corn and Special Seasonings; bring to a boil. Reduce heat to low. Cover; simmer 15 to 20 minutes or until rice is tender.

4. Stir in barbecue sauce and ground beef. Sprinkle with cheese. Cover; let stand 3 to 5 minutes or until cheese is melted.   *Makes 4 servings*

Prep Time: 5 minutes
Cook Time: 25 minutes

Salsa can be substituted for barbecue sauce.

RAGÚ® CHILI MAC

1 tablespoon olive or vegetable oil
1 medium green bell pepper, chopped
1 pound ground beef
1 jar (26 to 28 ounces) RAGÚ® Old World
    Style® Pasta Sauce
2 tablespoons chili powder
8 ounces elbow macaroni, cooked and
    drained

1. In 12-inch nonstick skillet, heat oil over medium-high heat and cook green bell pepper, stirring occasionally, 3 minutes. Add ground beef and brown, stirring occasionally; drain.

2. Stir in Ragú Pasta Sauce and chili powder. Bring to a boil over high heat. Reduce heat to low and simmer covered 10 minutes.

3. Stir in macaroni and heat through. Serve, if desired, with sour cream and shredded Cheddar cheese.   *Makes 4 servings*

Prep Time: 10 minutes
Cook Time: 25 minutes

JOE'S SPECIAL

Nonstick cooking spray
1 pound lean ground beef
2 cups sliced mushrooms
1 small onion, chopped
2 teaspoons Worcestershire sauce
1 teaspoon dried oregano leaves
1 teaspoon ground nutmeg
½ teaspoon garlic powder
½ teaspoon salt
1 package (10 ounces) frozen chopped
    spinach, thawed
4 large eggs, lightly beaten
⅓ cup grated Parmesan cheese

1. Spray large skillet with cooking spray. Add ground beef, mushrooms and onion; cook over medium-high heat 6 to 8 minutes or until onion is tender, breaking beef apart with wooden spoon. Add Worcestershire, oregano, nutmeg, garlic powder and salt. Cook until meat is no longer pink.

2. Drain spinach (do not squeeze dry); stir into meat mixture. Push mixture to one side of pan. Reduce heat to medium. Pour eggs into other side of pan; cook, without stirring, 1 to 2 minutes or until set on bottom. Lift eggs to allow uncooked portion to flow underneath. Repeat until softly set. Gently stir into meat mixture and heat through. Stir in cheese.

Makes 4 to 6 servings

Serving Suggestion: Serve with salsa and toast.

Prep and Cook Time: 20 minutes

Ragú® Chili Mac

ITALIAN BEEF BURRITO

1½ pounds ground beef
 2 medium onions, finely chopped
 2 medium red and/or green bell peppers, chopped
 1 jar (26 to 28 ounces) RAGÚ® Hearty Robusto!™ Pasta Sauce
 ½ teaspoon dried oregano leaves, crushed
 8 (10-inch) flour tortillas, warmed
 2 cups shredded mozzarella cheese (about 8 ounces)

1. In 12-inch skillet, brown ground beef over medium-high heat.

2. Stir in onions and red bell peppers and cook, stirring occasionally, 5 minutes or until tender; drain. Stir in Ragú Pasta Sauce and oregano; heat through.

3. To serve, top each tortilla with ¼ cup cheese and 1 cup ground beef mixture; roll up and serve. *Makes 8 servings*

Prep Time: 15 minutes
Cook Time: 15 minutes

GREEK BEEF & RICE

1 bag SUCCESS® Rice
 1 pound lean ground beef
 2 medium zucchini, sliced
 ½ cup chopped onion
 1 medium clove garlic, minced
 1 can (14½ ounces) tomato sauce
 ¾ teaspoon dried basil leaves, crushed
 ¾ teaspoon salt
 ¼ teaspoon pepper

Prepare rice according to package directions.

Brown beef in large skillet, stirring occasionally to separate beef. Pour off all but 2 tablespoons drippings. Add zucchini, onion and garlic to skillet; cook and stir until crisp-tender. Add all remaining ingredients *except* rice; cover. Simmer 10 minutes, stirring occasionally. Add rice; heat thoroughly, stirring occasionally. Garnish, if desired. *Makes 6 servings*

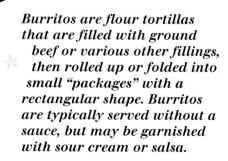

MAGIC TIP

Burritos are flour tortillas that are filled with ground beef or various other fillings, then rolled up or folded into small "packages" with a rectangular shape. Burritos are typically served without a sauce, but may be garnished with sour cream or salsa.

Italian Beef Burrito

PASTA BEEF & ZUCCHINI DINNER

1 pound extra lean ground beef
1 medium onion, chopped
1 clove garlic, crushed
½ teaspoon salt
2 (14-ounce) cans ready-to-serve beef broth
1 teaspoon Italian seasoning
¼ teaspoon crushed red pepper
2 cups uncooked mini lasagna or rotini pasta
2 cups sliced zucchini (cut ⅜ inch thick)
1 tablespoon cornstarch
¼ cup water
3 plum tomatoes, each cut into 4 wedges
2 tablespoons grated Parmesan cheese

In large nonstick skillet, cook ground beef with onion, garlic and salt over medium heat 8 to 10 minutes or until beef is browned, stirring occasionally to break up beef into 1-inch crumbles. Remove beef mixture with slotted spoon; set aside. Pour off drippings.

Add broth, Italian seasoning and red pepper to same skillet. Bring to a boil; add pasta. Reduce heat to medium; simmer, uncovered, for 6 minutes, stirring occasionally. Add zucchini; continue cooking an additional 6 to 8 minutes or until pasta is tender, yet firm. Push pasta and zucchini to side of skillet. Mix cornstarch with water and add to broth in skillet; bring to a boil. Return beef mixture to skillet. Add tomatoes; heat through, stirring occasionally. Spoon into serving dish; sprinkle with Parmesan cheese.

Makes 5 servings

*Favorite recipe from **North Dakota Wheat Commission***

CHEESEBURGER MACARONI

1 cup mostaccioli or elbow macaroni, uncooked
1 pound ground beef
1 medium onion, chopped
1 can (14½ ounces) DEL MONTE® Diced Tomatoes with Basil, Garlic & Oregano
¼ cup DEL MONTE® Tomato Ketchup
1 cup (4 ounces) shredded Cheddar cheese

1. Cook pasta according to package directions; drain.

2. Brown meat with onion in large skillet; drain. Season with salt and pepper, if desired. Stir in tomatoes, ketchup and pasta; heat through.

3. Top with cheese. Garnish, if desired.

Makes 4 servings

Prep Time: 8 minutes
Cook Time: 15 minutes

MAGIC TIP

To make chopping an onion a less tearful procedure, place the onion in the freezer for 15-20 minutes just before you begin. Also, do the chopping under a stove's exhaust fan, and try wearing some safety goggles purchased from a hardware store.

QUICK GREEK PITAS

1 pound ground beef
1 package (10 ounces) frozen chopped
    spinach, thawed and well drained
4 green onions, chopped
1 can (2¼ ounces) sliced black olives,
    drained
1 teaspoon dried oregano leaves, divided
¼ teaspoon black pepper
1 large tomato, diced
1 cup plain nonfat yogurt
½ cup mayonnaise
6 (6-inch) pita breads, warmed
    Lettuce leaves
1 cup (4 ounces) crumbled feta cheese

Cook and stir ground beef in large skillet over
medium-high heat until crumbly and no longer
pink. Drain off drippings. Add spinach, green
onions, olives, ½ teaspoon oregano and pepper;
cook and stir 2 minutes. Stir in tomato.

Combine yogurt, mayonnaise and remaining
½ teaspoon oregano in small bowl. Split open
pita breads; line each with lettuce leaf. Stir
cheese into beef mixture and divide among pita
pockets. Serve with yogurt sauce.

Makes 6 servings

SZECHWAN BEEF

1 pound ground beef
1 tablespoon vegetable oil
1 cup sliced carrots
1 cup frozen peas
⅓ cup water
3 tablespoons soy sauce
2 tablespoons cornstarch
¼ teaspoon ground ginger
1 jar (7 ounces) baby corn
1 medium onion, thinly sliced
    Sliced mushrooms and olives as desired
¼ cup shredded Cheddar cheese
1⅓ cups uncooked instant rice

1. In wok or large skillet, brown ground beef;
remove from wok and set aside. Drain fat.

2. Add oil to wok or skillet and return to
medium heat. Add carrots and peas and stir-fry
about 3 minutes.

3. In small cup, combine water and soy sauce
with cornstarch and ginger. Add to vegetables
in wok.

4. Return ground beef to wok along with baby
corn, onion, mushrooms, olives and cheese.
Cook over medium heat until all ingredients
are heated through.

5. Prepare instant rice according to package
directions. Serve beef and vegetables over rice.

Makes 4 to 5 servings

Favorite recipe from **North Dakota Beef Commission**

CURRY BEEF

12 ounces wide egg noodles *or* 1⅓ cups
    long-grain white rice
1 tablespoon olive oil
1 medium onion, thinly sliced
1 tablespoon curry powder
1 teaspoon ground cumin
2 cloves garlic, minced
1 pound lean ground beef
1 cup (8 ounces) sour cream
½ cup 2% milk
½ cup raisins, divided
1 teaspoon sugar
¼ cup chopped walnuts, almonds or
    pecans

1. Cook noodles or rice according to package directions. Meanwhile, heat oil in large skillet over medium-high heat until hot. Add onion; cook and stir 3 to 4 minutes. Add curry powder, cumin and garlic; cook 2 to 3 minutes longer or until onion is tender. Add meat; cook 6 to 8 minutes or until meat is no longer pink, breaking meat apart with wooden spoon.

2. Stir in sour cream, milk, ¼ cup raisins and sugar. Reduce heat to medium, stirring constantly, until heated through. Spoon over drained noodles or rice. Sprinkle with remaining ¼ cup raisins and nuts.

Makes 4 servings

Serving Suggestion: Serve with sliced cucumber sprinkled with sugar and vinegar or plain yogurt topped with brown sugar, chopped bananas and green onions.

Prep and Cook Time: 30 minutes

TEX-MEX BEEF & BLACK BEAN SKILLET

1 pound lean ground beef or ground
    turkey
1 medium onion, chopped
2 cloves garlic, minced
1 tablespoon Mexican seasoning*
1 (6.8-ounce) package RICE-A-RONI®
    Spanish Rice
2 tablespoons margarine or butter
1 (16-ounce) jar salsa *or* 1 (14½-ounce)
    can diced tomatoes and green chiles,
    undrained
1 (16-ounce) can black beans, rinsed and
    drained
1 cup shredded Monterey Jack cheese or
    jalapeño pepper

*1 teaspoon chili powder, 1 teaspoon ground cumin, 1 teaspoon garlic salt and ¼ teaspoon cayenne pepper may be substituted.

1. In large skillet over medium-high heat, cook ground beef, onion and garlic until meat is no longer pink, stirring frequently. Drain; transfer to bowl. Toss with Mexican seasoning; set aside.

2. In same skillet over medium heat, sauté rice-vermicelli mix with margarine until vermicelli is golden brown.

3. Slowly stir in 2 cups water, salsa and Special Seasonings; bring to a boil. Cover; reduce heat to low. Simmer 10 minutes.

4. Stir in beef mixture and beans. Cover; simmer 8 to 10 minutes or until rice is tender. Top with cheese. *Makes 6 servings*

Prep Time: 10 minutes
Cook Time: 25 minutes

Curry Beef

TACO POT PIE

1 pound ground beef
1 package (1.25 ounces) taco seasoning
    mix
¼ cup water
1 can (8 ounces) kidney beans, rinsed and
    drained
1 cup chopped tomato
¾ cup frozen corn, thawed
¾ cup frozen peas, thawed
1½ cups (6 ounces) shredded Cheddar
    cheese
1 package (11.5 ounces) refrigerated corn
    bread sticks

1. Preheat oven to 400°F. Brown beef in medium ovenproof skillet over medium-high heat, stirring to separate; drain drippings. Add seasoning mix and water to skillet. Cook over medium-low heat 3 minutes or until most of liquid is absorbed, stirring occasionally.

2. Stir in beans, tomato, corn and peas. Cook 3 minutes or until mixture is hot. Remove from heat; stir in cheese.

3. Unwrap corn bread dough; separate into 16 strips. Twist strips, cutting to fit skillet. Arrange attractively over meat mixture. Press ends of dough lightly to edges of skillet to secure. Bake 15 minutes or until corn bread is golden brown and meat mixture is bubbly.

Makes 4 to 6 servings

Prep and Cook Time: 30 minutes

WESTERN WAGON WHEELS

1 pound lean ground beef or ground
    turkey
2 cups wagon wheel pasta, uncooked
1 can (14½ ounces) stewed tomatoes
1½ cups water
1 box (10 ounces) BIRDS EYE® frozen
    Sweet Corn
½ cup barbecue sauce
    Salt and pepper to taste

• In large skillet, cook beef over medium heat 5 minutes or until well browned.

• Stir in pasta, tomatoes, water, corn and barbecue sauce; bring to a boil.

• Reduce heat to low; cover and simmer 15 to 20 minutes or until pasta is tender, stirring occasionally. Season with salt and pepper.

Makes 4 servings

Serving Suggestion: Serve with corn bread or corn muffins.

Prep Time: 5 minutes
Cook Time: 25 minutes

MAGIC TIP

For the best tomatoes, buy those that are firm and uniformly shaped, with a deep color and pleasant fragrance. Avoid those that feel heavy for their size, have any blemishes or seem too soft when gently palm-squeezed.

Taco Pot Pie

BROCCOLI AND BEEF PASTA

1 pound lean ground beef
2 cloves garlic, minced
1 can (about 14 ounces) beef broth
1 medium onion, thinly sliced
1 cup uncooked rotini pasta
½ teaspoon dried basil leaves
½ teaspoon dried oregano leaves
½ teaspoon dried thyme leaves
1 can (15 ounces) Italian-style tomatoes, undrained
2 cups broccoli florets *or* 1 package (10 ounces) frozen broccoli, thawed
3 ounces shredded Cheddar cheese or grated Parmesan cheese

1. Combine meat and garlic in large nonstick skillet; cook over high heat until meat is no longer pink, breaking meat apart with wooden spoon. Pour off drippings. Place meat in large bowl; set aside.

2. Add broth, onion, pasta, basil, oregano and thyme to skillet. Bring to a boil. Reduce heat to medium-high and boil 10 minutes (if using frozen broccoli, boil 15 minutes); add tomatoes with juice. Increase heat to high and bring to a boil; stir in broccoli. Cook, uncovered, 6 to 8 minutes, stirring occasionally, until broccoli is crisp-tender and pasta is tender. Return meat to skillet and stir 3 to 4 minutes or until heated through.

3. With slotted spoon, transfer to serving platter. Sprinkle with cheese. Cover with lid or tent with foil several minutes, until cheese melts. Meanwhile, bring liquid left in skillet to a boil over high heat. Boil until thick and reduced to 3 to 4 tablespoons. Spoon over pasta.

Makes 4 servings

Serving Suggestion: Serve with garlic bread.

Prep and Cook Time: 30 minutes

QUICK BEEF STROGANOFF

1 pound ground beef
1 package LIPTON® Noodles & Sauce— Butter
2¼ cups water
1 jar (4½ ounces) sliced mushrooms, drained
2 tablespoons finely chopped pimiento
⅛ teaspoon garlic powder
½ cup sour cream

In 10-inch skillet, brown ground beef; drain. Stir in remaining ingredients except sour cream. Bring to a boil, then simmer, stirring frequently, 7 minutes or until noodles are tender. Stir in sour cream; heat through but do not boil. *Makes about 2 servings*

Microwave Directions: In 2-quart microwavable casserole, cook ground beef at HIGH (Full Power) 4 to 6 minutes. Add noodles & sauce, butter, water, mushrooms, pimiento and garlic powder. Heat at HIGH 10 minutes or until noodles are tender, stirring occasionally. Stir in sour cream.

MAGIC TIP . . . .

Save time by using packaged preshredded Cheddar cheese and checking the salad bar at your supermarket for precut greens, toppers and trimmings.

Broccoli and Beef Pasta

PRESTO SOUPS, STEWS & CHILI

ALBÓNDIGAS SOUP

1 pound ground beef
¼ cup long-grain rice
1 egg
1 tablespoon chopped fresh cilantro
1 teaspoon LAWRY'S® Seasoned Salt
¼ cup ice water
2 cans (14½ ounces each) chicken broth
1 can (14½ ounces) whole peeled tomatoes, undrained and cut up
1 stalk celery, diced
1 large carrot, diced
1 medium potato, diced
¼ cup chopped onion
¼ teaspoon LAWRY'S® Garlic Powder with Parsley

In medium bowl, combine ground beef, rice, egg, cilantro, Seasoned Salt and ice water; mix well and form into small meatballs. In large saucepan, combine broth, vegetables and Garlic Powder with Parsley. Bring to a boil over medium-high heat; add meatballs. Reduce heat to low; cover and cook 30 to 40 minutes, stirring occasionally. *Makes 6 to 8 servings*

Serving Suggestion: Serve with lemon wedges and warm tortillas.

MAGIC TIP

For a lower-salt version, use homemade or low-sodium chicken broth.

HEARTY CHILI MAC

1 pound lean ground beef
1 can (14½ ounces) diced tomatoes,
    drained
1 cup chopped onion
1 clove garlic, minced
1 tablespoon chili powder
½ teaspoon salt
½ teaspoon ground cumin
½ teaspoon dried oregano leaves
¼ teaspoon black pepper
¼ teaspoon red pepper flakes
2 cups cooked macaroni

Crumble ground beef into slow cooker. Add remaining ingredients, except macaroni, to slow cooker. Cover and cook on LOW 4 hours. Stir in cooked macaroni. Cover and cook on LOW 1 hour.   *Makes 4 servings*

MAGIC TIP ....

To save time later in the week, double the pasta you make now. Simply drain the extra pasta, place it in ice water to stop further cooking, then drain it again. Toss with about a teaspoon of oil. Cover and refrigerate for up to 4 days.

....

MEXICAN VEGETABLE BEEF SOUP

1 pound ground beef
½ cup chopped onion
1 package (1.0 ounce) LAWRY'S® Taco
    Spices & Seasonings
1 can (28 ounces) whole tomatoes, cut up
1 package (16 ounces) frozen mixed
    vegetables, thawed
1 can (15¼ ounces) kidney beans,
    undrained
1 can (14½ ounces) beef broth
  Corn chips
  Shredded cheddar cheese

In Dutch oven, brown ground beef and onion, stirring until beef is crumbly and onion is tender; drain fat. Add Taco Spices & Seasonings, tomatoes, vegetables, beans and broth. Bring to a boil over medium-high heat; reduce heat to low and cook, uncovered, 5 minutes, stirring occasionally.   *Makes 6 servings*

Serving Suggestion: Top each serving with corn chips and shredded cheddar cheese.

Hint: For extra flavor, add chopped cilantro to beef mixture.

Hearty Chili Mac

TEXAS BEEF STEW

1 pound lean ground beef
1 small onion, chopped
1 can (28 ounces) crushed tomatoes with roasted garlic
1½ cups BIRDS EYE® frozen Farm Fresh Mixtures Broccoli, Cauliflower & Carrots
1 can (14½ ounces) whole new potatoes, halved
1 cup BIRDS EYE® frozen Sweet Corn
1 can (4½ ounces) chopped green chilies, drained
½ cup water

• In large saucepan, cook beef and onion over medium-high heat until beef is well browned, stirring occasionally.

• Stir in tomatoes, vegetables, potatoes with liquid, corn, chilies and water; bring to boil.

• Reduce heat to medium-low; cover and simmer 5 minutes or until heated through.

Makes 4 servings

Serving Suggestion: Serve over rice and with warm crusty bread.

Prep Time: 5 minutes
Cook Time: 15 minutes

QUICK & EASY CHILI

1 pound ground beef
1 cup (1 small) chopped onion
2 cloves garlic, finely chopped
3½ cups (two 15-ounce cans) kidney, pinto or black beans, drained
2½ cups (24-ounce jar) ORTEGA® Thick & Chunky Salsa, hot, medium or mild
½ cup (4-ounce can) ORTEGA® Diced Green Chiles
2 teaspoons chili powder
½ teaspoon dried oregano, crushed
½ teaspoon ground cumin
   Topping suggestions: ORTEGA® Thick and Chunky Salsa, shredded Cheddar cheese or Monterey Jack cheese, chopped tomatoes, sliced ripe olives, sliced green onions and sour cream

COOK beef, onion and garlic in large skillet over medium-high heat for 4 to 5 minutes or until beef is no longer pink; drain.

STIR in beans, salsa, chiles, chili powder, oregano and cumin. Bring to a boil. Reduce heat to low; cook, covered, for 20 to 25 minutes.

TOP as desired before serving.

Makes 6 servings

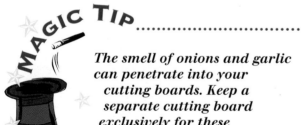

MAGIC TIP ....

The smell of onions and garlic can penetrate into your cutting boards. Keep a separate cutting board exclusively for these vegetables.

....

Texas Beef Stew

DURANGO CHILI

3 tablespoons vegetable oil, divided
1 pound lean ground beef
1 pound lean boneless beef, cut into
    ½-inch cubes
2 medium onions, chopped
1 green bell pepper, seeded and chopped
4 cloves garlic, minced
¼ cup tomato paste
3 to 5 fresh or canned jalapeño peppers,*
    stemmed, seeded and minced
2 bay leaves
5 tablespoons chili powder
1 teaspoon salt
1 teaspoon ground cumin
½ teaspoon black pepper
2 cans (14½ ounces each) tomatoes,
    undrained
1 bottle (12 ounces) beer
1 can (10¾ ounces) condensed beef broth
    plus 1 can water
2 cans (4 ounces each) diced green chilies,
    undrained
3 cups cooked pinto beans *or* 2 cans
    (15 ounces each) pinto or kidney
    beans, drained

CONDIMENTS
1 cup (4 ounces) shredded Cheddar cheese
½ cup sour cream
4 green onions with tops, thinly sliced
1 can (2¼ ounces) sliced pitted ripe olives,
    drained

Jalapeño peppers can sting and irritate the skin; wear rubber gloves when handling peppers and do not touch eyes. Wash hands after handling peppers.

Heat 1 tablespoon of the oil in 5-quart kettle over medium-high heat. Crumble in ground beef; add cubed beef. Cook, stirring occasionally, until meat is lightly browned. Transfer meat and pan drippings to a medium bowl. Heat the remaining 2 tablespoons oil in kettle over medium heat. Add onions, bell pepper and garlic. Cook until vegetables are tender. Stir in tomato paste, jalapeño peppers, bay leaves, chili powder, salt, cumin and black pepper. Coarsely chop tomatoes; add to kettle.

Add meat, beer, beef broth, water and green chilies. Bring to a boil. Reduce heat and simmer, partially covered, 2 hours or until meat is very tender and chili has thickened slightly. Stir in beans. Continue simmering, uncovered, 20 minutes. If you prefer thicker chili, continue simmering, uncovered, until chili is of desired consistency. Discard bay leaves. Spoon into individual bowls. Serve with condiments.

Makes 6 servings

HEARTY BEEF STEW

1 pound ground beef
1 tablespoon minced garlic
1 jar (14 ounces) marinara sauce
1 can (10½ ounces) condensed beef broth
1 package (16 ounces) Italian-style frozen
    vegetables
2 cups southern-style hash brown potatoes
2 tablespoons *French's*® Worcestershire
    Sauce
2 cups *French's*® *Taste Toppers*™ French
    Fried Onions

1. Brown beef with garlic in large saucepan until no longer pink; drain. Add marinara sauce, broth, vegetables, potatoes and Worcestershire. Bring to boiling; cover. Reduce heat to medium-low. Cook 10 minutes or until vegetables are crisp-tender.

2. Spoon soup into bowls. Sprinkle with *Taste Toppers*. Serve with garlic bread, if desired.

Makes 6 servings

Prep Time: 5 minutes
Cook Time: 15 minutes

HANOI BEEF AND RICE SOUP

1½ pounds ground chuck
2 tablespoons cold water
2 tablespoons soy sauce
2 teaspoons sugar
2 teaspoons cornstarch
2 teaspoons lime juice
½ teaspoon black pepper
2 cloves garlic, minced
2 teaspoons fennel seeds
1 teaspoon anise seeds
1 cinnamon stick (3 inches long)
2 bay leaves
6 whole cloves
1 tablespoon vegetable oil
1 cup uncooked long-grain white rice
1 medium yellow onion, sliced and
    separated into rings
1 tablespoon minced fresh ginger
4 cans (about 14 ounces each) beef broth
2 cups water
½ pound fresh snow peas, trimmed
1 fresh red Thai chili or red jalapeño
    pepper,* cut into slivers, for garnish

Thai chilies and jalapeño peppers can sting and irritate the skin; wear rubber gloves when handling chilies and do not touch eyes. Wash hands after handling peppers.

1. Combine beef, 2 tablespoons water, soy sauce, sugar, cornstarch, lime juice, black pepper and garlic in large bowl; mix well. Place meat mixture on cutting board; pat evenly into 1-inch-thick square. Cut meat into 36 squares; shape each square into a ball.

2. Bring 4 inches water to a boil in wok over high heat. Add meatballs and return water to a boil. Cook meatballs 3 to 4 minutes or until firm, stirring occasionally. Using a slotted spoon, transfer meatballs to bowl. Discard water.

3. Place fennel seeds, anise seeds, cinnamon, bay leaves and cloves on 12-inch double-thick square of dampened cheesecloth. Tie with string to create spice bag; set aside.

4. Heat wok over medium heat 1 minute or until hot. Drizzle oil into wok and heat 30 seconds. Add rice; cook and stir 3 to 4 minutes or until lightly browned. Add onion and ginger. Stir-fry 1 minute. Add beef broth, 2 cups water and spice bag. Cover and bring to a boil. Reduce heat to low; simmer 25 minutes.

5. Remove spice bag and discard. Add meatballs and snow peas to soup. Cook and stir until heated through. Ladle soup into tureen or individual serving bowls. Garnish, if desired.

Makes 6 main-dish servings

SPICY QUICK AND EASY CHILI

1 pound ground beef
1 large clove garlic, minced
1 can (15¼ ounces) DEL MONTE® Whole
    Kernel Golden Sweet Corn, drained
1 can (16 ounces) kidney beans, drained
1½ cups salsa, mild, medium or hot
1 can (4 ounces) diced green chiles,
    undrained

1. Brown meat with garlic in large saucepan; drain.

2. Add remaining ingredients. Simmer, uncovered, 10 minutes, stirring occasionally. Sprinkle with chopped green onions, if desired.

Makes 4 servings

Prep and Cook Time: 15 minutes

CLASSIC MEATBALL SOUP

2 pounds beef bones
3 ribs celery
2 carrots
1 medium onion, cut in half
1 bay leaf
6 cups cold water
1 egg
4 tablespoons chopped fresh parsley, divided
1 teaspoon salt, divided
½ teaspoon dried marjoram leaves, crushed
¼ teaspoon black pepper, divided
½ cup soft fresh bread crumbs
¼ cup grated Parmesan cheese
1 pound ground beef
1 can (14½ ounces) whole peeled tomatoes, undrained
½ cup uncooked rotini or small macaroni

1. To make stock, rinse beef bones and combine with celery, carrots, onion and bay leaf in 6-quart stockpot. Add water. Bring to a boil; reduce heat to low. Cover partially and simmer 1 hour, skimming foam occasionally.

2. Preheat oven to 400°F. Spray 13×9-inch baking pan with nonstick cooking spray. Combine egg, 3 tablespoons parsley, ½ teaspoon salt, marjoram and ⅛ teaspoon pepper in medium bowl; whisk lightly. Stir in bread crumbs and cheese. Add beef; mix well. Place meat mixture on cutting board; pat evenly into 1-inch-thick square. With sharp knife, cut meat into 1-inch squares; shape each square into a ball. Place meatballs in prepared pan; bake 20 to 25 minutes until brown on all sides and cooked through, turning occasionally. Drain on paper towels.

3. Strain stock through sieve into medium bowl. Slice celery and carrots; reserve. Discard bones, onion and bay leaf. To degrease stock, let stand 5 minutes to allow fat to rise. Holding paper towel, quickly pull across surface only, allowing towel to absorb fat. Discard. Repeat with clean paper towels as many times as needed to remove all fat.

4. Return stock to stockpot. Drain tomatoes, reserving juice. Chop tomatoes; add to stock with juice. Bring to a boil; boil 5 minutes. Stir in rotini, remaining ½ teaspoon salt and ⅛ teaspoon pepper. Cook 6 minutes, stirring occasionally. Add reserved vegetables and meatballs. Reduce heat to medium; cook 10 minutes or until hot. Stir in remaining 1 tablespoon parsley. Season to taste.

Makes 4 to 6 servings

CHILI BEEF MAC

1 pound lean ground beef or ground turkey
4 teaspoons Mexican seasoning*
⅔ cup milk
1 (4.8-ounce) package PASTA RONI® Four Cheese Flavor with Corkscrew Pasta
1 medium green, red or yellow bell pepper, diced
½ cup salsa
¼ cup chopped cilantro or sliced green onions

2 teaspoons chili powder, 1 teaspoon ground cumin and 1 teaspoon garlic salt may be substituted.

1. In large skillet over medium-high heat, cook ground beef and Mexican seasoning for 5 minutes, stirring occasionally.

2. Add 1¼ cups water, milk, pasta, bell pepper, salsa and Special Seasonings. Bring to a boil. Reduce heat to low. Cover; simmer 8 to 9 minutes or until pasta is tender. Stir in cilantro. Let stand 5 minutes before serving.

Makes 4 servings

Prep Time: 5 minutes
Cook Time: 20 minutes

Classic Meatball Soup

RAPID RAGÚ® CHILI

1½ pounds lean ground beef
1 medium onion, chopped
2 tablespoons chili powder
1 can (19 ounces) red kidney beans, rinsed and drained
1 jar (26 to 28 ounces) RAGÚ® Old World Style® Pasta Sauce
1 cup shredded Cheddar cheese (about 4 ounces)

1. In 12-inch skillet, brown ground beef with onion and chili powder over medium-high heat, stirring occasionally. Stir in beans and Ragú Pasta Sauce.

2. Bring to a boil over high heat. Reduce heat to low and simmer covered, stirring occasionally, 20 minutes. Top with cheese. Serve, if desired, over hot cooked rice.

Makes 6 servings

Prep Time: 10 minutes
Cook Time: 25 minutes

MAGIC TIP

Form meatballs easily and without a mess by spooning the beef mixture between sheets of plastic wrap and rolling into the desired shape.

MINESTRONE SOUP WITH MINI MEATBALLS

1 pound ground beef or ground turkey
1 teaspoon dried Italian seasoning
½ teaspoon garlic powder, divided
2 tablespoons vegetable oil, divided
5 cups assorted fresh vegetables*
1 envelope LIPTON® RECIPE SECRETS® Onion Soup Mix
4 cups water
1 can (28 ounces) Italian plum tomatoes, undrained
1 teaspoon sugar

*Use any of the following to equal 5 cups: green beans, cut into 1-inch pieces; diced zucchini; diced carrot; or diced celery.

In medium bowl, combine ground beef, Italian seasoning and ¼ teaspoon garlic powder. Shape into 1-inch meatballs.

In 6-quart Dutch oven or heavy saucepan, heat 1 tablespoon oil over medium-high heat and brown meatballs. Remove meatballs. Heat remaining 1 tablespoon oil in same Dutch oven and cook vegetables, stirring frequently, 5 minutes or until crisp-tender. Stir in soup mix blended with water, remaining ¼ teaspoon garlic powder, tomatoes and sugar. Bring to a boil over high heat, breaking up tomatoes with wooden spoon. Reduce heat to low and simmer covered 25 minutes. Return meatballs to skillet. Continue simmering covered 5 minutes or until meatballs are heated through. Serve with grated Parmesan cheese and garlic bread, if desired.

Makes 6 servings

Rapid Ragú® Chili

FARMER'S STEW ARGENTINA

3 cups water
1 pound lean ground beef
2 tablespoons vegetable oil
1 medium onion, chopped
1 green bell pepper, cut into ½-inch pieces
1 red bell pepper, cut into ½-inch pieces
1 small sweet potato, peeled and cut into ½-inch pieces
1 large clove garlic, minced
1 tablespoon chopped fresh parsley
1 teaspoon salt
½ teaspoon granulated sugar
⅛ teaspoon ground cumin
3 cups beef broth, heated
½ pound zucchini, cut into ½-inch pieces
1 cup whole kernel corn
2 tablespoons raisins
1 teaspoon TABASCO® brand Pepper Sauce
1 small pear, firm but ripe, cut into 1-inch pieces
6 cups cooked white rice

Bring water to a boil in large saucepan. Remove saucepan from heat. Add ground beef, stirring to break meat into little pieces. Let stand 5 minutes, stirring once or twice, until most of the pink disappears from meat. Drain meat well, discarding water.

Heat oil in large deep skillet or Dutch oven over medium-high heat. Add onion and cook 4 to 5 minutes, stirring constantly, until limp and slightly brown. Add beef. Continue cooking, stirring constantly, until all liquid has evaporated from pan and meat is lightly browned, about 10 minutes.

Reduce heat to medium. Add bell peppers, sweet potato and garlic. Continue cooking and stirring 5 minutes, or until peppers and potatoes are slightly tender. Add parsley, salt, sugar and cumin. Stir and cook 1 minute to blend flavors. Pour beef broth into skillet. Add zucchini, corn, raisins and TABASCO® Sauce. Simmer gently 10 minutes, being careful not to

boil. Add pear and simmer 10 additional minutes, or until all fruits and vegetables are tender. Ladle over rice in individual serving bowls.   *Makes 6 servings*

TEXAS-STYLE CHILI

1½ pounds ground beef or cubed round steak
1 green bell pepper, diced
1 onion, diced
1 can (2.25 ounces) diced green chiles, drained
1 package (1.48 ounces) LAWRY'S® Spices & Seasonings for Chili
1½ tablespoons cornmeal
1 tablespoon chili powder
1 teaspoon sugar
¼ to ½ teaspoon cayenne pepper
1 can (14½ ounces) diced tomatoes, undrained
¾ cup water
Sour cream (optional)
Shredded cheddar cheese (optional)

In Dutch oven or large saucepan, cook beef until browned and crumbly; drain beef, reserving fat; set beef aside. Cook bell pepper and onion in Dutch oven with reserved fat over medium-high heat 5 minutes or until vegetables are crisp-tender. Return beef to Dutch oven. Add chiles, Spices & Seasonings for Chili, cornmeal, chili powder, sugar and cayenne pepper; mix well. Stir in tomatoes and water. Bring to a boil over medium-high heat; reduce heat to low, cover and simmer 30 minutes, stirring occasionally.

Makes 4½ cups

Serving Suggestion: Serve topped with sour cream or cheddar cheese, if desired.

Hint: This recipe is perfect for leftover meat. Use 3½ cups shredded beef. If using shredded beef or cubed round steak, brown in 1 tablespoon vegetable oil.

WILD RICE SOUP

½ cup uncooked wild rice
1 pound lean ground beef
1 can (14½ ounces) chicken broth
1 can (10¾ ounces) condensed cream of
    mushroom soup
2 cups milk
1 cup (4 ounces) shredded Cheddar cheese
⅓ cup shredded carrot
1 package (.4 ounce) HIDDEN VALLEY®
    Buttermilk Recipe Original Ranch®
    salad dressing mix
Chopped green onions with tops

Cook rice according to package directions to make about 1½ cups cooked rice. In Dutch oven or large saucepan, brown beef; drain off excess fat. Stir in rice, chicken broth, cream of mushroom soup, milk, cheese, carrot and dry salad dressing mix. Heat to a simmer over low heat, stirring occasionally, about 15 minutes. Serve in warmed soup bowls; top with green onions. Garnish with additional green onions, if desired.
Makes 6 to 8 servings

MAGIC TIP

Avoid ground beef with a bad odor, discolored patches (usually gray or brown) or browned or dry-looking edges. When unsure if beef is fresh, apply the cook's saying: "If in doubt, throw it out."

MEATY CHILI

1 pound coarsely ground beef
¼ pound ground Italian sausage
1 large onion, chopped
2 medium ribs celery, diced
2 fresh jalapeño peppers,* chopped
2 cloves garlic, minced
1 can (28 ounces) whole peeled tomatoes,
    undrained, cut up
1 can (15 ounces) pinto beans, drained
1 can (12 ounces) tomato juice
1 cup water
¼ cup ketchup
1 teaspoon sugar
1 teaspoon chili powder
½ teaspoon salt
½ teaspoon ground cumin
½ teaspoon dried thyme leaves
⅛ teaspoon black pepper

Jalapeño peppers can sting and irritate the skin; wear rubber gloves when handling peppers and do not touch eyes. Wash hands after handling.

Cook beef, sausage, onion, celery, jalapeños and garlic in 5-quart Dutch oven over medium-high heat until meat is browned and onion is tender, stirring frequently.

Stir in tomatoes with liquid, beans, tomato juice, water, ketchup, sugar, chili powder, salt, cumin, thyme and black pepper. Bring to a boil over high heat. Reduce heat to medium-low; simmer, uncovered, 30 minutes, stirring occasionally.

Ladle into bowls. Garnish, if desired.
Makes 6 servings

ALL-IN-ONE BURGER STEW

1 pound lean ground beef
2 cups frozen Italian vegetables
1 can (14½ ounces) chopped tomatoes
    with basil and garlic
1 can (about 14 ounces) beef broth
2½ cups uncooked medium egg noodles
    Salt

1. Cook meat in Dutch oven or large skillet over medium-high heat until no longer pink, breaking meat apart with wooden spoon. Drain drippings.

2. Add vegetables, tomatoes and broth; bring to a boil over high heat.

3. Add noodles; reduce heat to medium. Cover and cook 12 to 15 minutes or until noodles have absorbed liquid and vegetables are tender. Add salt and pepper to taste.   *Makes 6 servings*

For a special touch, sprinkle with chopped parsley before serving.

Tip: To complete this meal, serve with breadsticks or a loaf of Italian bread and a mixed green and tomato salad.

Prep and Cook Time: 25 minutes

RIVERBOAT CHILI

2 pounds lean ground beef
2 large onions, chopped
1 large green pepper, chopped
2 cans (14½ ounces each) FRANK'S® or
    SNOWFLOSS® Original Style Diced
    Tomatoes, undrained
1 can (14½ ounces) FRANK'S® or
    SNOWFLOSS® Stewed Tomatoes,
    undrained
⅓ cup MISSISSIPPI® Barbecue Sauce
2 bay leaves
3 whole cloves
2 teaspoons chili powder
½ teaspoon cayenne pepper
½ teaspoon paprika
4 cans (15½ ounces each) dark red kidney
    beans

1. Brown ground beef in large stock pot. Drain grease.

2. Add onions, green pepper, diced tomatoes, stewed tomatoes, barbecue sauce, bay leaves, cloves, chili powder, cayenne pepper and paprika. Stir well.

3. Add kidney beans and stir well.

4. Cover and simmer 2 hours, stirring occasionally.   *Makes 4 to 6 servings*

Microwave Directions: Crumble beef into large microwavable casserole dish. Cook uncovered about 6 minutes, stirring at least twice to break up meat. Drain grease. Add onions, green pepper, diced tomatoes, stewed tomatoes, barbecue sauce, bay leaves, cloves, chili powder, cayenne pepper and paprika. Cook 1 minute. Stir well. Add kidney beans and stir well. Cover and cook 15 to 20 minutes, stirring occasionally. Cover and let stand 5 minutes.

Prep Time: 30 minutes
Cook Time: 2 hours

All-in-One Burger Stew

IN A FLASH

SALISBURY STEAKS WITH MUSHROOM-WINE SAUCE

   1 pound lean ground beef sirloin
   ¾ teaspoon garlic salt or seasoned salt
   ¼ teaspoon black pepper
   2 tablespoons butter or margarine
   1 package (8 ounces) sliced button mushrooms or 2 packages (4 ounces each) sliced exotic mushrooms
   2 tablespoons sweet vermouth or ruby port wine
   1 jar (12 ounces) or 1 can (10½ ounces) beef gravy

1. Heat large heavy nonstick skillet over medium-high heat 3 minutes or until hot.* Meanwhile, combine ground sirloin, garlic salt and pepper; mix well. Shape mixture into four ¼-inch-thick oval-shaped patties.

2. Place patties in skillet as they are formed; cook 3 minutes per side or until browned and heated through. Transfer to plate. Pour off drippings.

3. Melt butter in skillet; add mushrooms. Cook and stir 2 minutes. Add vermouth; cook 1 minute. Add gravy; mix well.

4. Return patties to skillet; simmer, uncovered, over medium heat 2 minutes for medium or until desired doneness, turning meat and stirring sauce.

Makes 4 servings

If pan is not heavy, use medium heat.

Note: For a special touch, sprinkle steaks with chopped parsley or chives.

Prep and Cook Time: 20 minutes

CRUNCHY LAYERED BEEF & BEAN SALAD

1 pound ground beef or turkey
2 cans (15 to 19 ounces *each*) black beans
  or pinto beans, rinsed and drained
1 can (14½ ounces) stewed tomatoes,
  undrained
1½ cups *French's® Taste Toppers*™ French
  Fried Onions, divided
1 package (1¼ ounces) taco seasoning mix
1 tablespoon *Frank's® RedHot®* Sauce
6 cups shredded lettuce
1 cup (4 ounces) shredded Cheddar or
  Monterey Jack cheese

1. Cook beef in large nonstick skillet over medium heat until thoroughly browned; drain well. Stir in beans, tomatoes, *½ cup Taste Toppers*, taco seasoning and *RedHot* Sauce. Heat to boiling. Cook over medium heat 5 minutes, stirring occasionally.

2. Spoon beef mixture over lettuce on serving platter. Top with cheese.

3. Microwave remaining *1 cup Taste Toppers* 1 minute on HIGH. Sprinkle over salad.

Makes 6 servings

Ultimate Pretzel Dip: Combine ½ cup *French's®* Honey Mustard **Grill & Glaze** Sauce with *French's® Classic Yellow Mustard®*, Dijon or Deli Mustard. Use for dipping pretzels, chips or cheese cubes.

Prep Time: 10 minutes
Cook Time: 6 minutes

SONOMA BURGERS STUFFED WITH BLUE CHEESE

½ pound ground beef or meat of your
  choice
  Salt and pepper
1 tablespoon Worcestershire sauce
2 ounces blue cheese, divided
8 SONOMA® Marinated Tomatoes,
  chopped
½ medium yellow onion, finely chopped

Season meat lightly with salt and pepper. Mix in Worcestershire sauce; halve the meat mixture and form into two patties. Carve a cavity into the center of each patty, stuff with blue cheese and reseal the patty exterior to keep cheese inside. Set aside.

Heat a non-stick skillet over medium-high heat until hot. Heat marinated tomatoes with some of their oil and the onion until mixture sizzles. Push mixture aside and add the two patties; let meat sear to seal in juices, then reduce heat to medium. Cover pan; cook 2 to 2½ minutes on each side. Add a pinch more of salt and pepper during last minutes of cooking. Serve each burger on toasted bread, if desired. Garnish with tomatoes and onions.

Makes 2 servings

Prep Time: 5 minutes
Cooking Time: 8 minutes

Crunchy Layered Beef & Bean Salad

FAST 'N' EASY CHILI

1½ pounds ground beef
  1 envelope LIPTON® RECIPE SECRETS®
    Onion Soup Mix*
  1 can (15 to 19 ounces) red kidney or black
    beans, drained
1½ cups water
  1 can (8 ounces) tomato sauce
  4 teaspoons chili powder

*Also terrific with LIPTON® RECIPE SECRETS® Beefy
Mushroom, Onion-Mushroom, Beefy Onion or Fiesta Herb
with Red Pepper Soup Mix.*

1. In 12-inch skillet, brown ground beef over
medium-high heat; drain.

2. Stir in remaining ingredients. Bring to a boil
over high heat. Reduce heat to low and simmer
covered, stirring occasionally, 20 minutes.
Serve, if desired, over hot cooked rice.

Makes 6 servings

First Alarm Chili: Add 5 teaspoons chili
powder.

Second Alarm Chili: Add 2 tablespoons chili
powder.

Third Alarm Chili: Add chili powder at your
own risk.

CREAMY BEEF AND VEGETABLE CASSEROLE

1 pound lean ground beef
1 small onion, chopped
1 bag (16 ounces) BIRDS EYE® frozen
    Farm Fresh Mixtures Broccoli, Corn
    & Red Peppers
1 can (10¾ ounces) cream of mushroom
    soup

• In medium skillet, brown beef and onion;
drain excess fat.

• Meanwhile, in large saucepan, cook
vegetables according to package directions;
drain.

• Stir in beef mixture and soup. Cook over
medium heat until heated through.

Makes 4 servings

Serving Suggestion: Serve over rice and
sprinkle with ½ cup shredded Cheddar cheese.

Prep Time: 5 minutes
Cook Time: 10 to 15 minutes

MAGIC TIP

*Keep spices fresh by storing
them in airtight containers
kept in a dark, cool place for
up to 6 months. Chili powder
and other spice blends should
never be kept over a stove or
other warm area, as they will
lose their flavor sooner.*

SLOPPY JOE ROLLERS

1 small onion, finely chopped
¼ cup finely chopped red bell pepper
1½ pounds ground beef
¾ cup chili sauce
2 tablespoons *French's*® Worcestershire
   Sauce
1⅓ cups *French's*® *Taste Toppers*™ French
   Fried Onions
1 cup shredded Cheddar cheese
8 (10-inch) flour tortillas, heated

1. Heat *1 tablespoon oil* in 12-inch nonstick skillet over medium-high heat. Cook onion and red pepper 2 minutes. Stir in meat and cook 5 minutes or until browned; drain. Stir in chili sauce and Worcestershire. Simmer 3 minutes.

2. To serve, arrange meat mixture, *Taste Toppers* and cheese down center of tortillas, dividing evenly. Fold bottom third of each tortilla over filling; fold sides towards center. Tightly roll up to secure filling. Cut in half to serve. *Makes 8 servings*

Prep Time: 5 minutes
Cook Time: 10 minutes

QUICK 'N' EASY TACOS

1 pound ground beef
1 can (14½ ounces) whole peeled
   tomatoes, undrained and coarsely
   chopped
1 medium green bell pepper, finely
   chopped
1 envelope LIPTON® RECIPE SECRETS®
   Onion Soup Mix*
1 tablespoon chili powder
3 drops hot pepper sauce (optional)
8 taco shells
   Taco Toppings

*Also terrific with Lipton® Recipe Secrets® Onion-Mushroom or Beefy Mushroom Soup Mix.

In medium skillet, brown ground beef over medium-high heat; drain. Stir in tomatoes, green pepper, onion soup mix, chili powder and hot pepper sauce, if using. Bring to a boil, then simmer 15 minutes or until slightly thickened. Serve in taco shells with assorted Taco Toppings. *Makes 4 servings*

Taco Toppings: Use shredded Cheddar or Monterey Jack cheese, shredded lettuce, chopped tomatoes, sliced pitted ripe olives, sour cream or taco sauce.

MINI MEXICAN BURGER BITES

1½ pounds ground beef
  ½ cup finely chopped red, yellow or green
    bell pepper
  2 tablespoons *French's*® Worcestershire
    Sauce
  1 teaspoon *Frank's*® *RedHot*® Sauce
  1 teaspoon dried oregano leaves
  ¼ teaspoon salt
 12 mini dinner rolls
    Shredded Cheddar cheese

1. Gently combine all ingredients except rolls
and cheese in large bowl. Shape into 12 mini
patties. Broil or grill patties 4 to 6 minutes for
medium doneness (160°F internal
temperature), turning once.

2. Arrange burgers on rolls and top with
Cheddar cheese. Top with shredded lettuce,
if desired.   *Makes 6 servings*

Prep Time: 5 minutes
Cook Time: 8 minutes

TACO TATERS

1 pound ground beef
1 jar (26 to 28 ounces) RAGÚ® Old World
  Style® Pasta Sauce
1 package (1.25 ounces) taco seasoning
  mix
6 large all-purpose potatoes, unpeeled and
  baked

1. In 12-inch skillet, brown ground beef over
medium-high heat; drain. Stir in Ragú Pasta
Sauce and taco seasoning mix and cook
5 minutes.

2. To serve, cut a lengthwise slice from top of
each potato. Evenly spoon beef mixture onto
each potato. Garnish, if desired, with shredded
Cheddar cheese and sour cream.
                              Makes 6 servings

Prep Time: 5 minutes
Cook Time: 15 minutes

Mini Mexican Burger Bites

SWEET AND SOUR BEEF

1 pound lean ground beef
1 small onion, thinly sliced
2 teaspoons minced fresh ginger
1 package (16 ounces) frozen mixed
 vegetables (snap peas, carrots, water
 chestnuts, pineapple, red pepper)
6 to 8 tablespoons bottled sweet and sour
 sauce or sauce from vegetable mix
 Cooked rice

1. Place beef, onion and ginger in large skillet; cook over high heat 6 to 8 minutes or until no longer pink, breaking apart with wooden spoon. Drain drippings.

2. Stir in frozen vegetables and sauce. Cook, covered, 6 to 8 minutes, stirring every 2 minutes or until vegetables are heated through. Serve over rice.   *Makes 4 servings*

Serving Suggestion: Serve with sliced Asian apple-pears.

Prep and Cook Time: 15 minutes

MAGIC TIP

Squeezing small chunks of peeled fresh ginger root in a garlic press is a fast and easy way to get minced ginger.

GROOVY ANGEL HAIR GOULASH

1 pound lean ground beef
2 tablespoons margarine or butter
1 (4.8-ounce) package PASTA RONI® Angel
 Hair Pasta with Herbs
1 (14½-ounce) can diced tomatoes,
 undrained
1 cup frozen or canned corn, drained

1. In large skillet over medium-high heat, brown ground beef. Remove from skillet; drain. Set aside.

2. In same skillet, bring 1½ cups water and margarine to a boil.

3. Stir in pasta; cook 1 minute or just until pasta softens slightly. Stir in tomatoes, corn, beef and Special Seasonings; return to a boil. Reduce heat to medium. Gently boil, uncovered, 4 to 5 minutes or until pasta is tender, stirring frequently. Let stand 3 to 5 minutes before serving.   *Makes 4 servings*

Prep Time: 5 minutes
Cook Time: 15 minutes

Sweet and Sour Beef

SPEEDY BEEF & BEAN BURRITOS

8 (7-inch) flour tortillas
1 pound ground beef
1 cup chopped onion
1 teaspoon bottled minced garlic
1 can (15 ounces) black beans, drained
    and rinsed
1 cup spicy thick and chunky salsa
2 teaspoons ground cumin
1 bunch cilantro
2 cups (8 ounces) shredded cojack or
    Monterey Jack cheese

1. Wrap tortillas in foil; place on center rack in oven. Heat oven to 350°F; heat tortillas 15 minutes.

2. While tortillas are warming, prepare burrito filling. Combine beef, onion and garlic in large skillet; cook over medium-high heat until beef is no longer pink, breaking beef apart with wooden spoon. Pour off drippings.

3. Stir beans, salsa and cumin into beef mixture; reduce heat to medium. Cover and simmer 10 minutes, stirring once.

4. While filling is simmering, chop enough cilantro to measure ¼ cup. Stir into filling. Spoon filling down centers of warm tortillas; top with cheese. Roll up and serve immediately.

Makes 4 servings

Prep and Cook Time: 20 minutes

BISTRO BURGERS WITH BLUE CHEESE

1 pound ground beef or turkey
¼ cup chopped fresh parsley
2 tablespoons minced chives
¼ teaspoon dried thyme leaves
2 tablespoons *French's®* Dijon Mustard
    Lettuce and tomato slices
4 crusty rolls, split in half
2 ounces blue cheese, crumbled
1⅓ cups *French's® Taste Toppers™* French
    Fried Onions

1. In large bowl, gently mix meat, herbs and mustard. Shape into 4 patties.

2. Grill or broil patties 10 minutes or until no longer pink in center. Arrange lettuce and tomatoes on bottom halves of rolls. Place burgers on top. Sprinkle with blue cheese and *Taste Toppers*. Cover with top halves of rolls. Serve with additional mustard.

Toast *Taste Toppers* in microwave 1 minute for extra crispness. *Makes 4 servings*

Prep Time: 10 minutes
Cook Time: 10 minutes

Speedy Beef & Bean Burritos

BITE SIZE TACOS

1 pound ground beef
1 package (1.25 ounces) taco seasoning
  mix
2 cups *French's® Taste Toppers™* French
  Fried Onions
¼ cup chopped fresh cilantro
32 bite size round tortilla chips
¾ cup sour cream
1 cup shredded Cheddar cheese

1. Cook beef in nonstick skillet over medium-high heat 5 minutes or until browned; drain. Stir in taco seasoning mix, *¾ cup water, 1 cup Taste Toppers* and cilantro. Simmer 5 minutes or until flavors are blended, stirring often.

2. Preheat oven to 350°F. Arrange tortilla chips on foil-lined baking sheet. Top with beef mixture, sour cream, remaining *Taste Toppers* and cheese.

3. Bake 5 minutes or until cheese is melted and *Taste Toppers* are golden.

Makes 8 appetizer servings

Prep Time: 5 minutes
Cook Time: 15 minutes

CORNY SLOPPY JOES

1 pound lean ground beef or ground
  turkey
1 small onion, chopped
1 can (15½ ounces) sloppy joe sauce
1 box (10 ounces) BIRDS EYE® frozen
  Sweet Corn
6 hamburger buns

• In large skillet, cook beef and onion over high heat until beef is well browned.

• Stir in sloppy joe sauce and corn; reduce heat to low and simmer 5 minutes or until heated through.

• Serve mixture in hamburger buns.

Makes 6 servings

Serving Suggestion: Sprinkle with shredded Cheddar cheese.

Prep Time: 5 minutes
Cook Time: 15 minutes

WESTERN HASH

1 pound ground beef
1 can (28 ounces) tomatoes, undrained
1 cup long-grain rice, uncooked
1 cup chopped green pepper
½ cup chopped onion
½ pound (8 ounces) VELVEETA®
    Pasteurized Prepared Cheese Product,
    sliced

BROWN meat in large skillet on medium-high heat; drain.

ADD tomatoes, rice, green pepper and onion; cover. Reduce heat to medium-low; simmer 25 minutes.

TOP with VELVEETA; continue cooking until VELVEETA is melted.   *Makes 6 servings*

Prep Time: 10 minutes

MAGIC TIP

To store fresh salsa, cover it tightly and refrigerate for up to 4 days. In addition to adding an exciting, spicy flavor to many Southwestern dishes, it can be used as a tasty topping for scrambled eggs, hash browns or hamburgers.

NACHO BACHO

1½ pounds ground beef
1 cup chunky hot salsa
½ cup salad dressing
2 tablespoons Italian seasoning
1 tablespoon chili powder
2 cups (8 ounces) shredded Colby-Jack
    cheese
3 cups nacho-flavored tortilla chips,
    crushed
1 cup sour cream
½ cup sliced black olives

Brown ground beef in skillet over medium heat; drain. In medium bowl, combine salsa, salad dressing, Italian seasoning and chili powder. Add beef. Place in 11×7-inch baking dish. Top with 1 cup cheese. Cover with crushed chips and remaining cheese. Bake at 350°F 20 minutes. Garnish with sour cream and sliced olives.   *Makes 4 servings*

Favorite recipe from **North Dakota Beef Commission**

BEEFY BEAN & WALNUT STIR-FRY

1 teaspoon vegetable oil
3 cloves garlic, minced
1 pound lean ground beef or ground
  turkey
1 bag (16 ounces) BIRDS EYE® frozen Cut
  Green Beans, thawed
1 teaspoon salt
½ cup walnut pieces

• In large skillet, heat oil and garlic over medium heat about 30 seconds.

• Add beef and beans; sprinkle with salt. Mix well.

• Cook 5 minutes or until beef is well browned, stirring occasionally.

• Stir in walnuts; cook 2 minutes more.

Makes 4 servings

Serving Suggestion: Serve over hot cooked egg noodles or rice.

Birds Eye® Idea: When you add California walnuts to Birds Eye® vegetables, you not only add texture and a great nutty taste, but nutrition, too.

Prep Time: 5 minutes
Cook Time: 7 to 10 minutes

TERIYAKI BURGERS

1 pound ground beef
3 tablespoons *French's*® Teriyaki Grill
  & Glaze Sauce

1. Combine beef with **Grill & Glaze** Sauce. Shape into 4 burgers.

2. Broil or grill burgers 10 minutes or until no longer pink in center, basting with additional **Grill & Glaze** Sauce. *Makes 4 servings*

Prep Time: 5 minutes
Cook Time: 15 minutes

Beefy Bean & Walnut Stir-Fry

RICE-STUFFED PEPPERS

1 package LIPTON® Rice & Sauce—
  Cheddar Broccoli
2 cups water
1 tablespoon margarine or butter
1 pound ground beef
4 large red or green bell peppers, halved
  lengthwise and seeded

Preheat oven to 350°F.

Prepare rice & sauce—cheddar broccoli with water and margarine according to package directions.

Meanwhile, in 10-inch skillet, brown ground beef over medium-high heat; drain. Stir into rice & sauce. Fill each pepper half with rice mixture. In 13×9-inch baking dish, arrange stuffed peppers. Bake covered 20 minutes. Remove cover and continue baking 10 minutes or until peppers are tender. Sprinkle, if desired, with shredded cheddar cheese.

Makes about 4 main-dish servings

MAGIC TIP ....

Select bell peppers that are firm and heavy in proportion to their size, with shiny skin and a robust color. Avoid peppers with wrinkled or limp skin, soft spots or bruises.

MAIN-DISH PIE

1 package (8 rolls) refrigerated crescent
  rolls
1 pound lean ground beef
1 medium onion, chopped
1 can (12 ounces) beef or mushroom gravy
1 box (10 ounces) BIRDS EYE® frozen
  Green Peas, thawed
½ cup shredded Swiss cheese
6 slices tomato

• Preheat oven to 350°F.

• Unroll dough and separate rolls. Spread to cover bottom of ungreased 9-inch pie pan. Press together to form lower crust. Bake 10 minutes.

• Meanwhile, in large skillet, brown beef and onion; drain excess fat.

• Stir in gravy and peas; cook until heated through.

• Pour mixture into partially baked crust. Sprinkle with cheese.

• Bake 10 to 15 minutes or until crust is brown and cheese is melted.

• Arrange tomato slices over pie; bake 2 minutes more.   *Makes 6 servings*

Prep Time: 10 minutes
Cook Time: 20 to 25 minutes

Contents

Soups 162

Salads 178

Main 194

Sides 212

Sauces 228

Soups

Tomato and Turkey Soup with Pesto

1 cup uncooked rotini pasta
2 cups (8 ounces) frozen Italian-style vegetables
1 can (10¾ ounces) reduced-sodium tomato soup
1 cup fat-free (skim) milk
2 tablespoons prepared pesto
1 cup coarsely chopped skinless cooked turkey
2 tablespoons grated Parmesan cheese

1. Cook pasta according to package directions, omitting salt. Drain and rinse well under cold water until pasta is cool; drain well.

2. Meanwhile, combine vegetables, soup, milk and pesto in medium saucepan. Bring to a boil over medium heat; reduce heat to low. Simmer, covered, 10 minutes or until vegetables are tender. Add pasta and turkey. Cook 3 minutes or until heated through. Sprinkle with cheese just before serving. *Makes 4 servings*

Tortellini Vegetable Soup

1 package (14 ounces) turkey or pork breakfast sausage, crumbled
2 quarts water
6 HERB-OX® Beef Bouillon cubes*
½ teaspoon garlic powder
1 package (9 ounces) fresh tortellini cheese pasta
1 package (16 ounces) frozen vegetable combination (broccoli, cauliflower, red pepper), thawed

*1 bouillon cube = 1 teaspoon instant bouillon = 1 packet instant broth and seasoning.

In Dutch oven over medium-high heat, cook sausage until browned; drain. Add water, bouillon and garlic powder; bring to a boil. Add pasta; boil 5 minutes. Stir in vegetables. Simmer, uncovered, 10 minutes or until vegetables and pasta are tender. *Makes 8 servings*

Five-Way Cincinnati Chili

    1 pound uncooked spaghetti, broken in half
    1 pound ground chuck
    2 cans (10 ounces each) tomatoes and green chilies, undrained
    1 can (15 ounces) red kidney beans, drained
    1 can (10½ ounces) condensed French onion soup
 1¼ cups water
    1 tablespoon chili powder
    1 teaspoon sugar
 ½ teaspoon salt
 ¼ teaspoon ground cinnamon
 ½ cup chopped onion
 ½ cup (2 ounces) shredded Cheddar cheese

1. Cook pasta according to package directions; drain.

2. While pasta is cooking, cook beef in large saucepan or Dutch oven over medium-high heat until browned, stirring to separate; drain well. Add tomatoes with juice, beans, soup, water, chili powder, sugar, salt and cinnamon to saucepan; bring to a boil. Reduce heat to low. Simmer uncovered, 10 minutes, stirring occasionally.

3. Serve chili over spaghetti; sprinkle with onion and cheese.

Makes 6 servings

Tuscany Chicken Soup

 4½ cups water
    1 package LIPTON® Noodles & Sauce—Chicken Flavor
    1 package (8 ounces) frozen Italian vegetables, partially thawed
    1 can (14½ ounces) whole peeled tomatoes, undrained and chopped
 1½ teaspoons garlic powder
    1 teaspoon dried oregano leaves
    2 cups cut-up cooked chicken
 ¼ cup grated Parmesan cheese
    Salt and ground black pepper to taste

In 3-quart saucepan, bring water to a boil. Stir in Noodles & Sauce—Chicken Flavor, vegetables, tomatoes, garlic powder and oregano. Cover and return to a boil. Uncover and continue boiling over medium heat, stirring occasionally, 8 minutes or until noodles and vegetables are tender. Stir in remaining ingredients and heat through.

Makes about 4 (2-cup) servings

Five-Way Cincinnati Chili

Quick Beef Soup

1½ **pounds lean ground beef**
1 **cup chopped onion**
2 **cloves garlic, finely chopped**
1 **can (28 ounces) tomatoes, undrained**
6 **cups water**
6 **beef bouillon cubes**
¼ **teaspoon black pepper**
1½ **cups frozen peas, carrots and corn vegetable blend**
½ **cup uncooked orzo**
   French bread (optional)

Cook beef, onion and garlic in large saucepan over medium-high heat until beef is brown, stirring to separate meat; drain fat.

Purée tomatoes with juice in covered blender or food processor. Add tomatoes, water, bouillon cubes and pepper to meat mixture. Bring to a boil; reduce heat to low. Simmer, uncovered, 20 minutes. Add vegetables and orzo. Simmer 15 minutes more. Serve with French bread. *Makes 6 servings*

Favorite recipe from **North Dakota Beef Commission**

Creamy Cheddar Cheese Soup

2 **cans (10¾ ounces each) condensed Cheddar cheese soup**
3 **cups milk or water**
3 **cups cooked vegetables, such as cauliflower, carrots and asparagus, cut into bite-size pieces**
2 **cups cooked medium shell pasta**
1⅓ **cups *French's*® *Taste Toppers*™ French Fried Onions**

Combine soup and milk in large saucepan. Stir in vegetables and pasta. Bring to a boil. Reduce heat. Cook until heated through, stirring often.

Place **Taste Toppers** on microwavable dish. Microwave on HIGH 1 minute or until **Taste Toppers** are golden.

Ladle soup into individual bowls. Sprinkle with **Taste Toppers**.

Makes 6 servings

Prep Time: 10 minutes   **Cook Time:** 5 minutes

Primavera Tortellini en Brodo

2 cans (about 14 ounces each) reduced-sodium chicken broth
1 package (9 ounces) refrigerated fresh tortellini (cheese, chicken or sausage)
2 cups frozen mixed vegetables, such as broccoli, green beans, onions and red bell peppers
1 teaspoon dried basil leaves
    Dash hot pepper sauce or to taste
2 teaspoons cornstarch
1 tablespoon water
¼ cup grated Romano or Parmesan cheese

1. Pour broth into large deep skillet. Cover and bring to a boil over high heat. Add tortellini; reduce heat to medium-high. Cook, uncovered, until pasta is tender, stirring occasionally. (Check package directions for approximate timing.)

2. Transfer tortellini to medium bowl with slotted spoon; keep warm.

3. Add vegetables, basil and hot pepper sauce to broth; bring to a boil. Reduce heat to medium; simmer about 3 minutes or until vegetables are crisp-tender.

4. Blend cornstarch and water in small cup until smooth. Stir into broth mixture. Cook about 2 minutes or until liquid thickens slightly, stirring frequently. Return tortellini to skillet; heat through. Ladle into shallow soup bowls; sprinkle with cheese.

Makes 2 servings

Serving Suggestion: Serve with salad and crusty Italian bread.

Prep and Cook Time: 20 minutes

Pantry Soup

   2 teaspoons olive oil
   8 ounces boneless skinless chicken, cubed
   2 cans (14.5 ounces each) CONTADINA® Diced Tomatoes with Italian Herbs,
       undrained
   ¾ cup chicken broth
   ¾ cup water
   1 cup garbanzo beans, undrained
   1 cup kidney beans, undrained
   1 package (16 ounces) frozen mixed vegetables
   ½ cup dry pasta (rotini or rotelle), cooked and drained
   2 teaspoons lemon juice

1. Heat oil in 5-quart saucepan with lid; sauté chicken about 3 to 4 minutes or until cooked, stirring occasionally.

2. Mix in tomatoes, broth, water, garbanzo and kidney beans; cover and bring to a boil. Add mixed vegetables and pasta; bring to a boil.

3. Reduce heat; cover and simmer 3 minutes or until vegetables are tender. Stir in lemon juice; serve with condiments, if desired.   *Makes 6 to 8 servings*

Optional Condiments: Grated Parmesan cheese, chopped fresh basil or parsley, or croutons.

Pesto & Tortellini Soup

   1 package (9 ounces) fresh cheese tortellini
   3 cans (about 14 ounces each) chicken broth
   1 jar (7 ounces) roasted red peppers, drained and slivered
   ¾ cup frozen green peas
   3 to 4 cups fresh spinach, washed and stems removed
   1 to 2 tablespoons pesto *or* ¼ cup grated Parmesan cheese

1. Cook tortellini according to package directions; drain.

2. While pasta is cooking, bring broth to a boil over high heat in covered Dutch oven. Add cooked tortellini, peppers and peas; return broth to a boil. Reduce heat to medium and simmer 1 minute.

3. Remove soup from heat; stir in spinach and pesto.   *Makes 6 servings*

Prep and Cook Time: 14 minutes

White Cheddar Seafood Chowder

     2 tablespoons margarine or butter
     ½ cup chopped onion
  2¼ cups water
     1 package (6.2 ounces) PASTA RONI® Shells & White Cheddar
     1 cup sliced carrots
     ½ teaspoon salt (optional)
     ¾ pound fresh or thawed frozen firm white fish, cut into ½-inch pieces
  1¼ cups milk
     2 tablespoons chopped parsley (optional)

1. In 3-quart saucepan, melt margarine over medium heat. Add onion; sauté 1 minute.

2. Add water; bring to a boil over high heat.

3. Stir in pasta, carrots and salt.

4. Bring just to a boil. Reduce heat to medium. Boil, uncovered, stirring frequently, 12 minutes.

5. Add fish, milk, parsley and Special Seasonings. Continue cooking 3 to 4 minutes, stirring occasionally, or until pasta is desired tenderness and fish is opaque.

Makes 4 servings

Chicken Tortellini Soup

     1 can (49½ ounces) chicken broth
     1 package PERDUE® SHORT CUTS® Fresh Italian Carved Chicken Breast
     1 package (9 ounces) fresh pesto or cheese tortellini or tortelloni
     1 cup fresh spinach or arugula leaves, shredded
     ¼ to ½ cup grated Parmesan cheese

In large saucepan over medium-high heat, bring broth to a boil. Add chicken and tortellini; cook 6 to 8 minutes, until pasta is tender, reducing heat to keep a gentle boil. Just before serving, stir in fresh spinach. Ladle soup into bowls and sprinkle with Parmesan cheese.

Makes 4 servings

Prep Time: 5 minutes   **Cook Time:** 15 minutes

Long Soup

1½ tablespoons vegetable oil
¼ of small head of cabbage, shredded
8 ounces boneless lean pork, cut into thin strips
6 cups chicken broth
2 tablespoons soy sauce
½ teaspoon minced fresh ginger
8 green onions with tops, diagonally cut into ½-inch slices
4 ounces Chinese-style thin egg noodles

1. Heat oil in wok or large skillet over medium-high heat. Add cabbage and pork; stir-fry until pork is no longer pink in center, about 5 minutes.

2. Add chicken broth, soy sauce and ginger. Bring to a boil. Reduce heat to low; simmer 10 minutes, stirring occasionally. Stir in onions.

3. Add noodles; cook just until noodles are tender, 2 to 4 minutes.

Makes 4 servings

Chicken Rotini Soup

½ pound boneless skinless chicken breasts, cut into ½-inch pieces
1 cup water
2 tablespoons butter or margarine
4 ounces fresh mushrooms, sliced
½ medium onion, chopped
4 cups chicken broth
1 teaspoon Worcestershire sauce
¼ teaspoon dried tarragon leaves, crushed
¾ cup uncooked rotini
1 small zucchini
Fresh basil for garnish

Combine chicken and water in medium saucepan. Bring to a boil over high heat. Reduce heat to medium-low; simmer 2 minutes. Drain water and rinse chicken. Melt butter in 5-quart Dutch oven or large saucepan over medium heat. Add mushrooms and onion. Cook and stir until onion is tender. Stir in chicken, chicken broth, Worcestershire and tarragon. Bring to a boil over high heat. Stir in uncooked pasta. Reduce heat to medium-low; simmer, uncovered, 5 minutes. Cut zucchini into ⅛-inch slices; halve any large slices. Add to soup; simmer, uncovered, about 5 minutes, or until pasta is tender. Ladle into bowls. Garnish, if desired.

Makes 4 servings

Onion Soup with Pasta

Nonstick cooking spray
3 cups sliced onions
3 cloves garlic, minced
$\frac{1}{2}$ teaspoon sugar
2 cans (14$\frac{1}{2}$ ounces each) reduced-sodium beef broth
$\frac{1}{2}$ cup uncooked small pasta stars
2 tablespoons dry sherry
$\frac{1}{4}$ teaspoon salt
$\frac{1}{8}$ teaspoon black pepper
Grated Parmesan cheese

1. Spray large saucepan with cooking spray; heat over medium heat until hot. Add onions and garlic. Cook, covered, 5 to 8 minutes or until onions are wilted. Stir in sugar; cook about 15 minutes or until onion mixture is very soft and browned.

2. Add broth to saucepan; bring to a boil. Add pasta and simmer, uncovered, 6 to 8 minutes or until tender. Stir in sherry, salt and pepper. Ladle soup into bowls; sprinkle lightly with Parmesan cheese. *Makes 4 servings*

Minute Minestrone Soup

$\frac{1}{2}$ pound turkey sausage, cut into small pieces
2 cloves garlic, crushed
3 cans (14$\frac{1}{2}$ ounces *each*) low-sodium chicken broth
2 cups frozen Italian blend vegetables
1 can (15 ounces) white kidney beans, rinsed and drained
1 can (14$\frac{1}{2}$ ounces) Italian stewed tomatoes, undrained
1 cup cooked ditalini or small shell pasta ($\frac{1}{2}$ cup uncooked)
3 tablespoons *French's*® Worcestershire Sauce

1. In medium saucepan, stir-fry sausage and garlic 5 minutes or until sausage is cooked; drain. Add broth, vegetables, beans and tomatoes. Heat to boiling. Simmer, uncovered, 5 minutes or until vegetables are crisp-tender.

2. Stir in pasta and Worcestershire. Cook until heated through. Serve with grated cheese and crusty bread, if desired. *Makes 6 servings*

Prep Time: 10 minutes   **Cook Time:** about 10 minutes

Onion Soup with Pasta

Pasta e Fagioli

1 teaspoon olive oil
3 cloves garlic, minced
1 can (15 ounces) cannellini or Great Northern beans, rinsed and drained
2 cans (about 14 ounces each) fat-free reduced-sodium chicken broth
½ cup white wine, divided
1 tablespoon dried basil leaves
½ teaspoon black pepper
¼ to ½ teaspoon red pepper flakes
6 ounces uncooked ditalini pasta or other small tube pasta
4 teaspoons grated Parmesan cheese

Heat oil in large saucepan over medium-low heat until hot. Add garlic and beans; cook and stir 3 minutes. Add chicken broth, ¼ cup wine, basil, black pepper and red pepper flakes. Bring to a boil over medium-high heat. Add pasta; cook 10 to 12 minutes or until tender. Add remaining ¼ cup wine just before pasta is fully cooked. Sprinkle with grated cheese. Serve immediately.

Makes 4 (1-cup) servings

Note: This soup will be very thick.

Italian Fish Soup

4 ounces fresh halibut or haddock steak (1 inch thick)
1 cup meatless spaghetti sauce
¾ cup fat-free reduced-sodium chicken broth
¾ cup water
1 teaspoon dried Italian seasoning
¾ cup uncooked small pasta shells
1½ cups frozen vegetable blend, such as broccoli, carrots and water chestnuts, or broccoli, carrots and cauliflower

1. Remove skin from fish. Cut fish into 1-inch pieces. Cover and refrigerate until needed.

2. Combine spaghetti sauce, broth, water and Italian seasoning in medium saucepan. Bring to a boil. Stir in pasta. Return to a boil. Reduce heat and simmer, covered, 5 minutes.

3. Stir in fish and frozen vegetables. Return to a boil. Reduce heat and simmer, covered, 4 to 5 minutes or until fish flakes easily when tested with fork and pasta is tender.

Makes 2 servings

Salads

Pepperoni Pasta Salad

1 package (16 ounces) BARILLA® Castellane, cooked according to package
    directions
½ red onion, chopped
½ green pepper, chopped
6 ounces sliced pepperoni, cut into quarters
4 ounces shredded Cheddar cheese
1 small tomato, cubed
½ small can chopped black olives
¾ cup Italian salad dressing

1. Thoroughly rinse castellane in cold water; drain and place in large serving bowl.
Add remaining ingredients except salad dressing.

2. About 1 hour before serving, add salad dressing and toss to coat. Toss again just
before serving, adding additional salad dressing if necessary.

Makes 8 to 10 servings

Pasta Pesto Salad

8 ounces BARILLA® Penne or Mostaccioli, cooked according to package
    directions and chilled
1 container (about 7 ounces) prepared pesto sauce
4 plum tomatoes, cut into large chunks
1 cup roasted red peppers, cut into strips*
1 cup (4 ounces) crumbled feta cheese
    Salt and pepper

*Roasted red peppers are available in jars in Italian, deli or produce sections of
supermarkets.*

1. Combine chilled penne and pesto sauce in large serving bowl.

2. Add tomatoes and red peppers; toss gently. Sprinkle with cheese. Add salt and
pepper to taste.

Makes 6 to 8 servings

Mediterranean Orzo Salad

SALAD
- 1 cup orzo pasta
- 1 cup diced red bell pepper
- ½ cup crumbled feta cheese
- 1 can (2¼ ounces) sliced ripe olives, rinsed and drained
- ¼ cup chopped fresh basil *or* ½ teaspoon dried basil
  Fresh basil leaves or parsley sprigs, for garnish (optional)

DRESSING
- 1 packet (1 ounce) HIDDEN VALLEY® Original Ranch® Salad Dressing
  & Recipe Mix
- 3 tablespoons olive oil
- 3 tablespoons red wine vinegar
- 1 teaspoon sugar

Cook orzo according to package directions, omitting salt. Rinse with cold water and drain well. Mix orzo, bell pepper, cheese, olives and chopped fresh basil in a large bowl. (If using dried basil, add to dressing.) Whisk together salad dressing & recipe mix, oil, vinegar and sugar. Stir dressing into orzo mixture. Cover and refrigerate at least 2 hours. Garnish with basil leaves before serving, if desired.

Makes 4 to 6 servings

Garden Pasta Salad

- 1 package (9 ounces) fresh tri-color rotini or shell macaroni
- 1 pint cherry tomatoes, halved
- 1 zucchini, chopped
- ¼ to ⅓ cup Italian dressing
- ¼ cup chopped fresh parsley
- ⅛ teaspoon black pepper

Cook pasta in lightly salted boiling water according to package directions; drain. Place pasta, tomatoes and zucchini in serving bowl. Add enough dressing to moisten; toss lightly. Add parsley and pepper; toss lightly. Serve warm.

Makes 4 servings

Mediterranean Orzo Salad

Nutty Caesar Salad Pasta

1 package (16 ounces) refrigerated angel hair pasta
⅓ cup slivered almonds
8 cups (about 10 ounces) prepared Italian salad blend (romaine and radicchio)
1¼ cups Caesar salad dressing
½ cup (2 ounces) grated Parmesan cheese
Black pepper
1 cup croutons

1. Preheat oven to 350°F. Cut pasta in half. Cook pasta according to package directions; drain well.

2. While pasta is cooking, spread almonds on baking sheet. Bake 3 minutes or until golden. Cool completely.

3. Combine pasta, almonds, salad blend, salad dressing and cheese in large bowl; toss to combine. Season to taste with pepper. Sprinkle with croutons. Serve warm.

Makes 4 servings

Prep and Cook Time: 17 minutes

Hidden Valley Ranch® Tortellini Salad

1 cup HIDDEN VALLEY® ORIGINAL RANCH® Dressing
9 ounces cheese tortellini, cooked and cooled
1 cup julienned ham
¾ cup frozen baby peas, thawed
½ cup Swiss cheese cubes
2 tablespoons minced green onions
1 tablespoon minced parsley

Toss all ingredients together in a bowl. Chill until ready to serve.

Makes 4 to 6 servings

Sicilian-Style Pasta Salad

1 pound dry rotini pasta
2 cans (14.5 ounces) CONTADINA® Recipe Ready Diced Tomatoes with
    Italian Herbs, undrained
1 cup sliced yellow bell pepper
1 cup sliced zucchini
8 ounces cooked bay shrimp
1 can (2.25 ounces) sliced pitted ripe olives, drained
2 tablespoons balsamic vinegar

1. Cook pasta according to package directions; drain.

2. Combine pasta, undrained tomatoes, bell pepper, zucchini, shrimp, olives and vinegar in large bowl; toss well.

3. Cover. Chill before serving.
Makes 10 servings

Fresh Orange-Pasta Salad

6 cups cooked pasta, drained (2 cups *each* of three types of pasta, such as
    bow ties, shaped and/or spaghetti twists)*
3 California-Arizona oranges, peeled and cut into half-cartwheel slices
1 cup cooked asparagus cut into 2-inch lengths**
¼ cup vegetable or salad oil
    Grated peel of ½ orange
2 tablespoons fresh squeezed orange juice
    Juice of ½ California-Arizona lemon
1 tablespoon honey
1 tablespoon Dijon mustard
    Salt and pepper to taste

Cook pasta according to package directions for time and amount to yield 2 cups each, cooked.

**Cooked green beans or broccoli flowerets can be substituted for asparagus.*

In large bowl, combine cooked pasta, orange half-cartwheel slices and asparagus. In small bowl, whisk together oil, orange peel and juice, lemon juice, honey and mustard. Pour over and mix well with pasta ingredients. Salt and pepper to taste. Chill. Toss well before serving.
Makes 8 servings (about 9 cups)

Taco Salad

3 ounces uncooked radiatore pasta, cooked and drained
½ cup frozen corn, thawed
½ cup chopped seeded tomato
1 can (4 ounces) diced mild green chilies, drained
¼ cup chopped onion
2 tablespoons sliced ripe olives
2 tablespoons chopped fresh cilantro
½ cup mild or medium chunky salsa
½ teaspoon chili powder

Combine pasta, corn, tomato, chilies, onion, olives and cilantro in large bowl. Combine salsa and chili powder in small bowl until well blended. Pour over pasta mixture; toss to coat. Cover; refrigerate 2 hours. Garnish, if desired.

Makes 6 servings

Favorite Macaroni Salad

8 ounces uncooked medium shell pasta
⅓ cup reduced-fat sour cream
⅓ cup reduced-fat mayonnaise
⅓ cup *French's*® Hearty Deli Brown Mustard
1 tablespoon cider vinegar
3 cups bite-sized fresh vegetables, such as tomatoes, peppers, carrots and celery
¼ cup minced green onions

1. Cook pasta according to package directions using shortest cooking time; rinse with cold water and drain.

2. Combine sour cream, mayonnaise, mustard and vinegar in large bowl. Add pasta, vegetables and green onions. Toss gently to coat evenly. Season to taste with salt and pepper. Cover; chill in refrigerator 30 minutes. Stir before serving.

Makes 6 (1-cup) servings

Note: Create German-style mustard by adding minced garlic to *French's*® Hearty Deli Brown Mustard.

Prep Time: 20 minutes   **Chill Time:** 30 minutes

Taco Salad

Caesar Shrimp Pasta Salad

1 can (14½ ounces) DEL MONTE® Diced Tomatoes with Garlic & Onion,
   undrained
1 pound cooked tiny shrimp
6 cups cooked shell or corkscrew pasta
1 small cucumber, diced
1 cup Caesar dressing
3 green onions, sliced

1. Drain tomatoes, reserving ⅓ cup liquid. In large bowl, combine reserved tomato liquid with tomatoes and remaining ingredients. Season with salt and pepper to taste, if desired.

2. Cover and refrigerate until serving time. Garnish, if desired.

Makes 4 servings

Prep Time: 10 minutes

Italian Pasta & Vegetable Salad

8 ounces uncooked rotelle or spiral pasta
2½ cups assorted cut-up fresh vegetables (broccoli, carrots, tomatoes, bell
   peppers, cauliflower, onions and mushrooms)
½ cup cubed cheddar or mozzarella cheese
⅓ cup sliced pitted ripe olives (optional)
1 cup WISH-BONE® Italian Dressing*

*Also terrific with WISH-BONE® Robusto Italian, Fat Free Italian, Ranch, Fat Free Ranch, Creamy Caesar and Red Wine Vinaigrette Dressing.

Cook pasta according to package directions; drain and rinse with cold water until completely cool.

In large bowl, combine all ingredients except Italian dressing. Add dressing; toss well. Serve chilled or at room temperature. *Makes 8 side-dish servings*

Note: If preparing a day ahead, refrigerate, then stir in ¼ cup additional Wish-Bone® Dressing before serving.

Caesar Shrimp Pasta Salad

Oriental Steak Salad

1 package (3 ounces) Oriental flavor instant ramen noodles, uncooked
4 cups water
1 bag (16 ounces) BIRDS EYE® frozen Farm Fresh Mixtures Cauliflower,
  Carrots & Snow Pea Pods
2 tablespoons vegetable oil
1 pound boneless beef top loin steak, cut into thin strips
⅓ cup Oriental sesame salad dressing
¼ cup chow mein noodles
  Lettuce leaves

• Reserve seasoning packet from noodles.

• In large saucepan, bring water to boil. Add ramen noodles and vegetables; return to boil and cook 5 minutes, stirring occasionally. Drain.

• Heat oil in large nonstick skillet over medium-high heat. Add beef; cook and stir about 8 minutes or until browned.

• Stir in reserved seasoning packet until beef is well coated.

• In large bowl, toss together beef, vegetables, ramen noodles and salad dressing. Sprinkle with chow mein noodles. Serve over lettuce.   *Makes 4 servings*

Serving Suggestion: Salad can also be served chilled. Moisten with additional salad dressing, if necessary. Sprinkle with chow mein noodles and spoon over lettuce just before serving.

Prep Time: 10 minutes   **Cook Time:** 12 to 15 minutes

Italian Vegetable Salad

1 package (9 ounces) DI GIORNO® Three Cheese Tortellini, cooked, drained
1 small zucchini, cut in half lengthwise, sliced
½ each green and red pepper, chopped
½ cup halved cherry tomatoes
½ cup prepared GOOD SEASONS® Reduced Calorie Italian or Zesty Italian
  Salad Dressing
2 green onions, diagonally sliced

TOSS all ingredients in large bowl; cover. Refrigerate at least 2 hours.

STIR in additional dressing just before serving, if desired.   *Makes 8 servings*

Prep: 10 minutes plus refrigerating

Roasted Tomato and Mozzarella Pasta Salad

3 cups (8 ounces) rotelle pasta, uncooked
3 cups Roasted Fresh Tomatoes (recipe follows)
1 cup green bell pepper, cut into ½-inch pieces
¾ cup (3 ounces) mozzarella cheese, cut into ½-inch pieces
¼ cup chopped mild red onion
½ teaspoon salt
¼ teaspoon black pepper
⅓ cup prepared red wine vinaigrette salad dressing

Cook pasta according to package directions; rinse and drain. Place pasta in large bowl. Cut Roasted Fresh Tomatoes into chunks; add to pasta. Add bell pepper, mozzarella, onion, salt and black pepper to pasta. Pour salad dressing over top; toss to combine. Garnish with fresh basil leaves, if desired.   *Makes 4 servings*

Favorite recipe from **Florida Tomato Committee**

Roasted Fresh Tomatoes

6 large (about 3 pounds) Florida tomatoes
2 tablespoons vegetable oil
½ teaspoon dried basil leaves
¼ teaspoon dried thyme leaves
¼ teaspoon salt
¼ teaspoon black pepper

Preheat oven to 425°F. Use tomatoes held at room temperature until fully ripe. Core tomatoes; cut into halves horizontally. Gently squeeze halves to remove seeds. Place cut side up on rack in broiler pan; set aside. Combine oil, basil, thyme, salt and pepper in small bowl; brush over cut sides of tomatoes. Place tomatoes cut side down on rack. Bake about 30 minutes or until well browned. Remove skins, if desired. Serve hot, warm or cold.   *Makes 4 to 6 servings*

Favorite recipe from **Florida Tomato Committee**

Antipasto Salad

1 cup **MIRACLE WHIP®** Salad Dressing
½ **cup milk**
2 **packages GOOD SEASONS® Italian Salad Dressing Mix**
1 **package (16 ounces) uncooked mostaccioli, cooked, drained**
1 **package (8 ounces) OSCAR MAYER® Cotto Salami Slices, cut into strips**
1 **package (8 ounces) KRAFT® Low-Moisture Part-Skim Mozzarella Cheese, cubed**
¾ **cup** *each* **thin red bell pepper strips and thin zucchini strips**
½ **cup pitted ripe olives, drained, halved**

• MIX salad dressing, milk, and salad dressing mix in large bowl.

• ADD pasta; mix lightly.

• ARRANGE remaining ingredients over pasta mixture; cover. Refrigerate several hours or overnight until chilled.   *Makes 10 to 12 servings*

Prep Time: 15 minutes plus refrigerating

Zesty Pasta Salad

3 **ounces uncooked tri-color rotini pasta**
1 **cup sliced mushrooms**
¾ **cup pasta-ready canned tomatoes, undrained**
½ **cup sliced green bell pepper**
¼ **cup chopped onion**
¼ **cup fat-free Italian salad dressing**
2 **tablespoons grated Parmesan cheese**

1. Cook pasta according to package directions, omitting salt. Rinse with cool water; drain. Cool.

2. Combine pasta, mushrooms, tomatoes with juice, bell pepper and onion in large bowl. Pour Italian dressing over pasta mixture; toss to coat.

3. Top with cheese before serving. Garnish with lettuce leaves, if desired.
Makes 6 servings

Main

Tuscan Chicken and Pasta

8 ounces BARILLA® Rotini
¼ cup chopped dry-pack sun-dried tomatoes
2 medium zucchini, cut into matchstick strips
1 tablespoon olive or vegetable oil
1 jar (26 ounces) BARILLA® Tomato and Basil Pasta Sauce
1 cup (about 5 ounces) cooked chicken strips (purchased ready-to-eat, frozen
    or homemade)
¼ cup (1 ounce) grated Parmesan cheese

1. Begin cooking rotini according to package directions. Add sun-dried tomatoes to pasta during last 5 minutes of cooking; drain rotini and tomatoes.

2. Meanwhile, combine zucchini and oil in large (6-cup or more) microwave-safe bowl; cover with plastic wrap. Microwave on HIGH 4 minutes, stirring twice.

3. Stir in pasta sauce and chicken. Cover with plastic wrap; microwave on HIGH 4 minutes, stirring twice. Combine sauce mixture, hot drained rotini with sun-dried tomatoes, and cheese; toss to coat. *Makes 6 to 8 servings*

Tip: Parmesan, a firm cheese, should be wrapped airtight in a plastic bag or foil and stored in the cheese compartment (or the warmest location) of your refrigerator for up to several weeks.

Tuna Mac

2 cups water
2 cups (8 ounces) elbow macaroni, uncooked
¾ pound (12 ounces) VELVEETA® Pasteurized Prepared Cheese Product, cut up
1 package (16 ounces) frozen vegetable blend, thawed, drained
1 can (6 ounces) tuna, drained, flaked
2 tablespoons milk

1. Bring water to boil in saucepan. Stir in macaroni. Reduce heat to medium-low; cover. Simmer 8 to 10 minutes or until macaroni is tender.

2. Add Velveeta, vegetables, tuna and milk; stir until Velveeta is melted.

Makes 4 to 6 servings

Prep Time: 10 minutes   **Cook Time:** 15 minutes

Broccoli Shrimp Pasta

8 ounces linguine
3 cups fresh broccoli
1 tablespoon butter
1 (8-ounce) package frozen medium shrimp, thawed*
¼ cup sherry cooking wine
3 tablespoons soy sauce
2 tablespoons sliced almonds
1 tablespoon sesame seeds

Or, substitute 2 cups cubed cooked chicken for shrimp.

Cook linguine according to package directions; drain.

Bring 2 quarts water to a boil. Place broccoli in water and cook 2 minutes; drain. Melt butter in skillet or wok. Sauté shrimp 2 minutes over medium-high heat. Add broccoli, sherry and soy sauce. Cook 2 minutes. Add almonds and stir.

Place linguine on serving tray. Spoon broccoli-shrimp mixture, including liquid, over top of linguine. Sprinkle with sesame seeds.

Makes 4 servings

Favorite recipe from **North Dakota Wheat Commission**

Beef Stroganoff

12 ounces wide egg noodles
1 can (10¾ ounces) condensed cream of mushroom soup
1 cup (8 ounces) sour cream
1 packet (1¼ ounces) dry onion soup mix
1¼ to 1½ pounds lean ground beef
½ (10-ounce) package frozen peas

1. Place 3 quarts water in 8-quart stock pot; bring to a boil over high heat. Stir in noodles; boil, uncovered, 6 minutes or until tender. Drain.

2. Meanwhile, place mushroom soup, sour cream and onion soup mix in medium bowl. Stir until blended; set aside. Place meat in large skillet; cook over high heat 6 to 8 minutes or until meat is no longer pink, stirring to separate. Pour off drippings. Reduce heat to low. Add soup mixture; stir over low heat until bubbly. Stir in peas; heat through. Serve over noodles. *Makes 6 servings*

Prep and Cook Time: 20 minutes

Italian Pasta Bake

1 pound ground beef *or* Italian sausage
4 cups cooked mostaccioli *or* penne pasta
1 jar (28 to 30 ounces) spaghetti sauce (about 2¾ cups)
¾ cup KRAFT® 100% Grated Parmesan Cheese, divided
2 cups KRAFT® Shredded Low-Moisture Part-Skim Mozzarella Cheese

BROWN meat in large skillet; drain.

STIR in mostaccioli, spaghetti sauce and ½ cup of the Parmesan cheese. Spoon into 13×9-inch baking dish. Top with mozzarella cheese and remaining ¼ cup Parmesan cheese.

BAKE at 375°F for 20 minutes. *Makes 6 servings*

Prep Time: 10 minutes   **Bake Time:** 20 minutes

Dressed Chicken Breasts with Angel Hair Pasta

 1 cup prepared HIDDEN VALLEY® Original Ranch® salad dressing
⅓ cup Dijon-style mustard
 4 whole chicken breasts, halved, skinned, boned and pounded thin
½ cup butter or margarine
⅓ cup dry white wine
10 ounces angel hair pasta, cooked and drained
   Chopped parsley

In small bowl, whisk together salad dressing and mustard; set aside. In medium skillet, sauté chicken in butter until browned; transfer to dish. Keep warm. Pour wine into skillet; cook over medium-high heat, scraping up any browned bits from bottom of skillet, about 5 minutes. Whisk in dressing mixture; blend well. Serve chicken with sauce over pasta; sprinkle with parsley. *Makes 8 servings*

Spaghetti with Fresh Tomato Sauce

2½ pounds fresh ripe tomatoes, peeled, seeded and chopped
25 imported black olives, pitted and chopped
 3 tablespoons olive oil
 2 cloves garlic, minced
½ teaspoon salt
½ teaspoon red pepper flakes
 1 package (16 ounces) BARILLA® Spaghetti
½ cup grated Romano cheese

1. Combine tomatoes, olives, olive oil, garlic, salt and red pepper flakes in serving bowl. Set aside for 30 minutes to allow flavors to blend.

2. Meanwhile, cook spaghetti according to package directions; drain.

3. Add spaghetti and cheese to serving bowl with tomato mixture; toss. Serve immediately. *Makes 6 to 8 servings*

Dressed Chicken Breast with Angel Hair Pasta

30-Minute Chili Mac

  1 (1-pound) beef top round steak, cut into ¼-inch-thick strips
½ cup chopped onion
  1 tablespoon vegetable oil
  1 (16-ounce) can whole tomatoes, undrained, coarsely chopped
½ cup A.1.® Original or A.1.® BOLD & SPICY Steak Sauce
  2 tablespoons chili powder
  1 cup uncooked elbow macaroni, cooked, drained
  1 cup drained canned kidney beans, optional
⅓ cup shredded Cheddar cheese (about 1½ ounces)
¼ cup chopped fresh cilantro

In large skillet, over medium heat, cook steak and onion in oil 8 to 10 minutes, stirring occasionally. Stir in tomatoes with liquid, steak sauce and chili powder. Heat to a boil; reduce heat. Cover; simmer 10 minutes or until steak is tender. Stir in macaroni and beans, if desired. Sprinkle with cheese and cilantro. Serve immediately.

Makes 4 servings

Cheesy Skillet Lasagna

  1 pound ground beef
  2 jars (14 ounces *each*) marinara sauce
  2 cups cooked rotini pasta
1⅓ cups *French's*® *Taste Toppers*™ French Fried Onions, divided
  1 cup ricotta cheese
  1 cup (4 ounces) shredded mozzarella cheese

1. Cook beef in large skillet until browned; drain. Stir in sauce, pasta and ⅔ cup **Taste Toppers**. Heat to boiling, stirring.

2. Spoon ricotta cheese over beef mixture. Sprinkle with mozzarella cheese and remaining ⅔ cup **Taste Toppers**. Cover; cook over medium-low heat 3 minutes or until cheese melts.

Makes 4 servings

Prep Time: 10 minutes   **Cook Time:** 10 minutes

Basil Shrimp Fettuccine

3 tablespoons butter
3 tablespoons olive oil
2 tomatoes, peeled, seeded and chopped
1 garlic clove, minced
⅓ cup evaporated skim milk
½ cup HOLLAND HOUSE® White Cooking Wine
½ cup fresh basil, chopped
½ cup shrimp, peeled and deveined
4 tablespoons Parmesan cheese, grated and divided
4 tablespoons fresh parsley, chopped and divided
1 pound fettuccine, cooked and drained

Melt butter and oil in medium saucepan over medium heat. Add tomatoes and garlic; simmer until tomatoes are softened. Add milk and cooking wine; simmer 10 minutes. Stir in basil and shrimp; simmer 3 minutes or until shrimp turn pink and are opaque. Add 2 tablespoons cheese and 2 tablespoons parsley. Serve over cooked fettuccine. Sprinkle with remaining 2 tablespoons each, cheese and parsley.

Makes 4 to 6 servings

Creamy Pasta Primavera

1 bag (16 ounces) BIRDS EYE® frozen Pasta Secrets Primavera
½ cup 1% milk
2 packages (3 ounces each) cream cheese, cubed
1 cup cubed ham
¼ cup grated Parmesan cheese

• In large skillet, heat Pasta Secrets in milk over medium heat to a simmer; cover and simmer 7 to 9 minutes or until vegetables are tender.

• Add cream cheese; reduce heat to low and cook until cream cheese is melted, stirring often.

• Stir in ham and cheese; cover and cook 5 minutes more.   *Makes 4 servings*

Prep Time: 10 minutes   **Cook Time:** 20 minutes

Pasta Fazool

2 tablespoons olive oil
1 cup chopped onions
½ cup *each:* sliced carrots and sliced celery
2 cloves garlic, minced
4 cups chicken broth
1 (15-ounce) can HUNT'S® Tomato Sauce
1 (15-ounce) can white kidney beans, drained
1 (14½-ounce) can HUNT'S® Choice-Cut Diced Tomatoes with Italian Style
   Herbs
1 (8-ounce) can red kidney beans, drained
½ cup uncooked elbow macaroni
2 tablespoons chopped fresh parsley
2 teaspoons fresh basil leaves
½ teaspoon *each:* dried oregano leaves and salt
¼ teaspoon black pepper
   Fresh grated Parmesan cheese

In Dutch oven, heat oil and sauté onions, carrots, celery and garlic until tender. Stir in remaining ingredients except Parmesan cheese. Bring to a boil; reduce heat and simmer 10 to 15 minutes or until macaroni is tender. Sprinkle Parmesan cheese over each serving. *Makes 10 servings*

Original Ranch® Tetrazzini

8 ounces linguine, cooked and drained
3 cups shredded cooked chicken
1½ cups HIDDEN VALLEY® ORIGINAL RANCH® Dressing
½ cup dry white wine or chicken broth
1 jar (4½ ounces) sliced mushrooms, drained
¼ cup buttered* bread crumbs

Melt 1½ teaspoons butter; stir in plain dry bread crumbs until evenly coated.

Combine linguine, chicken, dressing, wine and mushrooms. Pour into a 2-quart casserole dish. Top with crumbs. Bake at 350°F. for 20 minutes or until bubbly around edges. *Makes 6 servings*

Macaroni and Cheese Pronto

8 ounces uncooked elbow macaroni
1 can (10¾ ounces) cream of Cheddar soup
½ cup milk
2 cups diced cooked ham (about ½ pound)
1 cup (4 ounces) shredded Cheddar cheese
½ cup frozen green peas
Black pepper

1. Cook macaroni according to package directions. Drain and set aside.

2. While macaroni is cooking, combine soup and milk in medium saucepan. Cook and stir over medium heat until smooth.

3. Add ham, cheese, peas and cooked macaroni to soup mixture. Reduce heat to low; cook and stir 5 minutes or until cheese melts and mixture is heated through. Add pepper to taste. *Makes 4 servings*

Tip: For a special touch, garnish Macaroni and Cheese Pronto with fresh Italian parsley before serving.

Prep and Cook Time: 20 minutes

Garden Vegetable Linguine

8 ounces uncooked linguine
1 pound HILLSHIRE FARM® Smoked Sausage, sliced
5 green or red bell peppers, cut into strips
4 to 5 carrots, sliced
1 package (10 ounces) frozen peas
¾ cup pitted black olives
1 cup Italian salad dressing
Pinch garlic powder
Pinch dried oregano leaves

Cook linguine according to package directions; drain and keep warm. Sauté Smoked Sausage with peppers, carrots, peas and olives in large skillet over medium-high heat. Combine salad dressing, linguine and sausage mixture in large serving bowl. Toss with garlic powder and oregano. Serve hot or cold. *Makes 6 servings*

Greens and Gemelli

8 ounces BARILLA® Gemelli
1 tablespoon olive oil
1 bag (10 ounces) spinach, washed and trimmed
1 jar (26 ounces) BARILLA® Green & Black Olive Pasta Sauce
8 ounces Italian sausage, cooked and crumbled
¼ cup crumbled feta cheese

1. Cook gemelli according to package directions; drain.

2. Meanwhile, add olive oil to large skillet. Add spinach; cook and stir 1 minute over medium-high heat.

3. Reduce heat; stir in pasta sauce and cooked sausage. Cook 5 minutes.

4. Pour sauce over hot drained gemelli; sprinkle with cheese.

Makes 4 to 6 servings

Vegetable Almond Fettuccine

6 tablespoons butter or margarine
2 cloves garlic, minced
2 teaspoons dried basil leaves
1 teaspoon onion powder
2 cups heavy cream
¼ teaspoon salt
¼ teaspoon black pepper
1 package (9 ounces) fresh spinach fettucine
¾ pound yellow crookneck squash, thinly sliced
1 red bell pepper, coarsely chopped
⅔ cup slivered almonds
¼ cup grated Parmesan cheese

1. Melt butter in small nonstick skillet over high heat. Add garlic; reduce heat. Cook 1 minute. Remove from heat; stir in basil, onion powder, heavy cream, salt and black pepper. Keep warm.

2. Bring 3 quarts water to a boil in large saucepan. Add fettuccine, squash and bell pepper. Cook 3 minutes or until vegetables are crisp-tender. Drain; return to saucepan.

3. Pour butter sauce and almonds over fettuccine; toss. Transfer to serving bowl.

4. Sprinkle with cheese. Serve immediately. *Makes 3 to 4 servings*

Crispy Lemon Pepper Chicken
with Spinach Pasta

2 BUTTERBALL® Chicken Requests™ Lemon Pepper Crispy Baked Breasts
2 cups uncooked bow tie pasta
3 tablespoons water
1 tablespoon olive oil
6 cups fresh spinach
2 cloves garlic, minced
½ cup part skim ricotta cheese
   Grated Parmesan cheese (optional)

Prepare chicken according to package directions. Cook and drain pasta. Add water and oil to skillet. Add spinach; cover. Cook 2 to 4 minutes or until spinach is wilted. Stir in garlic and cooked pasta; continue cooking 2 minutes longer. Add ricotta cheese; stir to blend. Serve spinach pasta topped with sliced chicken breasts. Sprinkle with Parmesan cheese.   *Makes 2 servings*

Note: Chicken Requests™ Crispy Baked Breasts are available in 5 flavors: Original, Italian Style Herb, Parmesan, Southwestern and Lemon Pepper.

Preparation Time: 20 minutes

Seafood Pasta

1 pound imitation crab, cut into bite size pieces
1 jar (15 ounces) seafood sauce
1 can (15 ounces) VEG•ALL® Mixed Vegetables, drained
1 can (14½ ounces) diced tomatoes, with liquid
1 can (4 ounces) sliced mushrooms, drained
½ teaspoon dried thyme
½ teaspoon dried basil
¼ teaspoon dried oregano
1 package (7 ounces) uncooked spaghetti

1. In large saucepan, combine crab, sauce, Veg•All, tomatoes, mushrooms, thyme, basil and oregano. Heat over medium heat until hot.

2. Cook spaghetti according to package directions.

3. Serve crab mixture over cooked pasta.   *Makes 4 servings*

Crispy Lemon Pepper Chicken with Spinach Pasta

Sides

Ultimate Macaroni & Cheese

 2 cups (8 ounces) elbow macaroni, uncooked
 1 pound (16 ounces) VELVEETA® Pasteurized Prepared Cheese Product, cut up
 ½ cup milk
 Dash pepper

1. Cook macaroni as directed on package; drain well. Return to same pan.

2. Add Velveeta, milk and pepper to same pan. Stir on low heat until Velveeta is melted. Serve immediately.   *Makes 4 to 6 servings*

Prep Time: 5 minutes   **Cook Time:** 15 minutes

Asian Spaghetti

 3 tablespoons CRISCO® Oil,* divided
 ½ pound uncooked spaghetti
 3 tablespoons sesame seeds
 3 tablespoons soy sauce
 1 scallion or green onion, trimmed and thinly sliced

Use your favorite Crisco Oil product.

1. Bring large pot of salted water to a boil on high heat. Add 2 tablespoons oil and spaghetti. Boil according to package directions until al dente. Drain.

2. Heat remaining 1 tablespoon oil in small skillet on medium heat. Add sesame seeds. Sauté 2 minutes, or until brown.

3. Toss spaghetti with soy sauce, sesame seeds and scallion. Serve immediately.
Makes 4 servings

Preparation Time: 10 minutes   **Total Time:** 25 minutes

Ultimate Macaroni & Cheese

Pasta Primavera

2 tablespoons butter or margarine
1 medium onion, finely chopped
1 clove garlic, minced
¾ pound asparagus, cut diagonally into 1½-inch pieces
½ pound fresh mushrooms, sliced
1 medium zucchini, sliced
1 carrot, sliced
1 cup half-and-half or light cream
½ cup chicken broth
1 tablespoon all-purpose flour
2 teaspoons dried basil leaves, crushed
1 pound uncooked fettuccine
¾ cup (3 ounces) SARGENTO® Parmesan & Romano Blend Shredded Cheese

In large skillet over medium heat, melt butter. Add onion and garlic; cook and stir until onion is tender. Add asparagus, mushrooms, zucchini and carrot; cook, stirring constantly, 2 minutes. Increase heat to high. Combine half-and-half, broth, flour and basil in small bowl; add to skillet. Bring mixture to a boil. Boil, stirring occasionally, until thickened.

Meanwhile, cook fettuccine according to package directions; drain. In serving bowl, place hot fettuccine, sauce and cheese; toss gently.   *Makes 8 servings*

Linguine with Oil and Garlic

½ cup FILIPPO BERIO® Extra Virgin Olive Oil, divided
10 cloves garlic, minced
¾ pound uncooked linguine
¼ teaspoon black pepper
¼ teaspoon salt (optional)

1. Heat 2 tablespoons olive oil in small saucepan over medium heat. Add garlic; cook and stir until lightly browned. Remove from heat; set aside.

2. Cook linguine according to package directions until tender. Do not overcook.

3. Drain pasta; return to saucepan. Toss with garlic and olive oil mixture, remaining 6 tablespoons olive oil, pepper and salt, if desired.

Makes 4 servings

Pepperoni Pasta Salad

**1 bag (16 ounces) BIRDS EYE® frozen Farm Fresh Mixtures Broccoli, Red
    Peppers, Onions and Mushrooms
2 cups cooked penne or macaroni
1 package (3 ounces) thinly sliced pepperoni
¼ to ½ cup peppercorn or ranch salad dressing**

- Cook vegetables according to package directions; drain.

- Combine vegetables and pasta in large bowl. Chill.

- Toss with pepperoni and dressing. Add salt and pepper to taste.

Makes 4 to 6 servings

Prep Time: 2 minutes, plus chilling time   **Cook Time:** 10 to 12 minutes

Oriental Noodles

**1 tablespoon plus 1½ teaspoons vegetable oil
1 small green bell pepper, thinly sliced
1 small red bell pepper, thinly sliced
2 tablespoons soy sauce
2 teaspoons sesame oil
1 teaspoon brown sugar
½ teaspoon ground ginger
½ teaspoon LAWRY'S® Garlic Powder with Parsley
½ teaspoon LAWRY'S® Seasoned Pepper
6 ounces spaghetti or vermicelli, cooked, drained and kept hot**

In large skillet, heat oil. Add bell peppers and cook over medium-high heat until crisp-tender. Stir in soy sauce, sesame oil, brown sugar, ginger, Garlic Powder with Parsley and Seasoned Pepper; mix well. Add hot spaghetti; toss lightly to coat.

Makes 6 servings

Serving Suggestion: Serve with grilled poultry or meat.

Pasta with Zesty Tomato Pesto

1 jar (8 ounces) sun-dried tomatoes, in oil, undrained
⅓ cup *French's*® Hearty Deli Brown Mustard
¼ cup grated Parmesan cheese
2 tablespoons pine nuts or slivered almonds
1 tablespoon *French's*® *RedHot*® Cayenne Pepper Sauce
1 clove garlic, coarsely chopped
1 box (16 ounces) uncooked bow-tie pasta

1. Combine sun-dried tomatoes with oil, 1 cup water, mustard, Parmesan, pine nuts, **Frank's RedHot** and garlic in blender or food processor. Cover; process until well blended.

2. Cook pasta according to package directions; drain well. Place in large bowl. Pour sauce over pasta; toss well to coat evenly. Serve warm or at room temperature. *Makes 6 side-dish servings (2 cups pesto)*

Note: If you enjoy the taste of pesto sauce, try adding ¼ cup **French's**® Dijon Mustard to 1 cup prepared pesto to make a spicy pesto dip or spread.

Prep Time: 15 minutes   **Cook Time:** 10 minutes

Easy Cheesy Pastina

1 package (12 ounces) BARILLA® Egg Pastina
1 package (8 ounces) pasteurized process cheese spread
1 can (8 ounces) tomato sauce
½ cup milk
  Salt and pepper

1. Cook pastina according to package directions; drain.

2. Cut cheese into chunks. Place cheese, tomato sauce and milk in medium saucepan. Cook and stir over low heat until cheese is melted and mixture is smooth.

3. Remove saucepan from heat; stir in cooked pastina. Add salt and pepper to taste. *Makes 6 to 8 servings*

Pasta Waldorf

8 ounces uncooked small shell pasta
2 Red Delicious apples
1 rib celery
½ cup chopped pecans
½ cup chopped raisins
⅓ cup lemon nonfat yogurt
⅓ cup reduced-fat mayonnaise
Salt

1. Cook pasta according to package directions; drain. Rinse in cold water; drain again.

2. While pasta is cooking, peel, core and dice apples. Chop celery.

3. Combine pasta, apples, celery, pecans, raisins, yogurt and mayonnaise in large bowl. Toss gently until blended. Season to taste with salt. Cover and chill 5 minutes. *Makes 6 side-dish servings*

Prep/Cook/Chill Time: 20 minutes

Walnut Lemon Couscous

2 tablespoons olive oil
1 cup California walnut pieces
2 large cloves garlic, pressed
⅔ cup chicken bouillon or broth
¼ cup fresh lemon juice
½ cup sliced green onions
½ cup sliced, pitted ripe olives
4 thin lemon slices, quartered
¾ cup instant couscous
Salt and pepper, to taste

In 8- to 10-inch skillet heat oil over medium heat. Add walnuts and garlic; toss 2 minutes. Add bouillon, lemon juice, onions, olives and lemon pieces. Bring to boiling. Stir in couscous. Remove from heat; cover and set aside 5 minutes. Toss with fork; season with salt and pepper. Serve immediately with baked or broiled chicken. *Makes 4 servings (3 cups)*

Favorite recipe from **Walnut Marketing Board**

Pasta Waldorf

Mediterranean Orzo with Pesto

    1 package (16 ounces) BARILLA® Orzo
    1 container (about 7 ounces) prepared pesto sauce
    ½ cup (2 ounces) grated Parmesan cheese
    1 teaspoon red pepper flakes
    1 jar (6 ounces) marinated artichoke hearts, drained, cut in half
    ¾ cup pitted kalamata olives *or* 1 can (6 ounces drained weight) whole pitted small ripe olives, drained
    Salt and pepper

1. Cook orzo according to package directions; drain.

2. Combine orzo, pesto sauce, cheese and red pepper flakes in large bowl. Stir in artichokes, olives and salt and pepper to taste. Serve immediately.

Makes 8 to 10 servings

Szechuan Cold Noodles

    8 ounces vermicelli, broken in half, or Chinese egg noodles
    3 tablespoons rice vinegar
    3 tablespoons soy sauce
    2 tablespoons peanut or vegetable oil
    1 large clove garlic, minced
    1 teaspoon minced fresh ginger
    1 teaspoon dark sesame oil (optional)
    ½ teaspoon crushed Szechuan peppercorns or crushed red pepper
    ½ cup coarsely chopped fresh cilantro (optional)
    ¼ cup chopped peanuts

1. Cook vermicelli according to package directions; drain.

2. Combine vinegar, soy sauce, peanut oil, garlic, ginger, sesame oil, if desired, and peppercorns in large bowl. Add hot vermicelli; toss to coat. Sprinkle with cilantro, if desired, and peanuts. Serve at room temperature or chilled.

Makes 4 servings

Variation: For Szechuan Vegetable Noodles, add 1 cup chopped peeled cucumber, ½ cup *each* chopped red bell pepper and sliced green onions and an additional 1 tablespoon soy sauce.

Couscous with Vegetables in Savory Broth

  2 tablespoons margarine or butter
  1 large onion, sliced
  ½ cup dry white wine or water
  1 cup sliced carrots
  1 medium zucchini, sliced
  1 small red or green bell pepper, sliced
  1 envelope LIPTON® RECIPE SECRETS® Savory Herb with Garlic Soup Mix
  2 cups water
  1⅓ cups (8 ounces) couscous, cooked*

Variation: Use hot cooked penne or ziti pasta.

In 12-inch skillet, melt butter over medium heat and cook onion, stirring occasionally, 5 minutes or until golden. Add wine and boil over high heat 1 minute. Stir in carrots, zucchini, red pepper and savory herb with garlic soup mix blended with water. Bring to a boil over high heat. Reduce heat to low and simmer uncovered, stirring occasionally, 15 minutes. To serve, spoon over hot couscous.

Makes about 5 side-dish servings

Cheesy Shells

  1 package (16 ounces) BARILLA® Medium Shells
  ¾ cup (12 ounces) pasteurized prepared cheese, cubed
  1 cup heavy whipping cream
  1 teaspoon garlic powder
  1 teaspoon dry mustard
  1 teaspoon paprika
    Salt and pepper

1. Begin cooking pasta shells according to package directions.

2. Meanwhile, heat cheese and cream in medium saucepan over medium heat until cheese melts, stirring frequently. Stir in garlic, mustard and paprika.

3. Drain pasta shells; return to cooking pot. Pour cheese mixture over shells; stir to coat. Add salt and pepper to taste.

Makes 8 servings

Couscous with Vegetables in Savory Broth

Creamy Vegetables & Pasta

1 can (10¾ ounces) condensed cream of chicken soup
1 cup milk
¼ cup grated Parmesan cheese
1 package (16 ounces) frozen seasoned pasta and vegetable combination
1⅓ cups French's® Taste Toppers™ French Fried Onions, divided

Combine soup, milk and cheese in 2-quart microwaveable shallow casserole. Stir in vegetable combination and ⅔ cup **Taste Toppers**. Microwave on HIGH 12 minutes* or until vegetables and pasta are crisp-tender, stirring halfway through cooking time. Sprinkle with remaining ⅔ cup **Taste Toppers**. Microwave 1 minute or until **Taste Toppers** are golden.   *Makes 6 servings*

Or, bake in preheated 350°F oven 30 to 35 minutes.

Mini Penne with Mascarpone

1 package (16 ounces) BARILLA® Mini Penne
2 tablespoons melted butter
⅔ cup grated Parmesan cheese
⅓ cup fresh mascarpone (semi-soft cheese), cream cheese or goat cheese
½ cup finely chopped lean cooked ham

1. Cook penne according to package directions; drain and transfer to preheated serving bowl.

2. Add butter and Parmesan; mix well. Dot with pieces of mascarpone. Sprinkle with ham. Serve immediately.   *Makes 6 to 8 servings*

Sauces

Fresh 'n' Sassy Spaghetti Sauce

2 tablespoons olive oil
1 medium onion, diced
2 large cloves garlic, minced
5 cups chopped fresh tomatoes
½ cup coarsely chopped fresh basil leaves
1 teaspoon salt
1 teaspoon TABASCO® brand Pepper Sauce

Heat oil in 4-quart saucepan over medium heat. Add onion and garlic; cook 5 minutes, stirring occasionally. Add tomatoes, basil, salt and TABASCO® Sauce; heat to boiling over high heat. Reduce heat to low; simmer, uncovered, 15 minutes, stirring occasionally.   *Makes about 3 cups sauce*

Note: Recipe makes enough sauce to serve over one 16-ounce package spaghetti, cooked.

Pine Nut and Cilantro Pesto

1 cup pine nuts
½ cup cilantro leaves
½ teaspoon LAWRY'S® Garlic Powder with Parsley
¼ teaspoon LAWRY'S® Seasoned Salt
2 tablespoons water
1 tablespoon vegetable oil

In food processor, combine pine nuts, cilantro, Garlic Powder with Parsley and Seasoned Salt. Process until smooth. Add water and oil. Process until well blended.
Makes 2 servings

Serving Suggestion: Serve over hot pasta and sliced black olives.

Sun-Dried Tomato Pesto

1 cup fat-free reduced-sodium chicken broth
1 cup sun-dried tomato halves (not packed in oil), drained
½ cup chopped fresh parsley
3 tablespoons walnut pieces, divided
2 tablespoons Parmesan cheese
   Pasta, cooked and drained
   Grated Parmesan cheese (optional)

1. Bring chicken broth to a boil in small saucepan over high heat; remove from heat. Add sun-dried tomatoes; set aside 5 minutes.

2. Drain tomatoes, reserving liquid. Place tomatoes, parsley, 2 tablespoons walnuts, 2 tablespoons Parmesan cheese and ½ cup reserved liquid in food processor or blender; process until smooth, adding an additional 2 to 4 tablespoons reserved liquid as needed for desired consistency. Toss with pasta until well coated. Top with remaining 1 tablespoon walnuts and grated Parmesan cheese, if desired.

Makes 8 (2-tablespoon) servings

Wild Mushroom Sauce

3 tablespoons olive oil
12 ounces shiitake or porcini mushrooms, sliced
6 ounces cremini or button mushrooms, sliced
1½ cups sliced green onions and tops
1 tablespoon dried basil leaves
½ to 1 teaspoon dried thyme leaves
3 cups vegetable broth, divided
1½ tablespoons cornstarch
2 tablespoons minced parsley
½ teaspoon salt
4 to 6 dashes hot pepper sauce

Heat oil in large skillet over medium heat until hot. Add mushrooms, green onions, basil and thyme; cook and stir 5 minutes or until mushrooms release liquid. Continue cooking 10 minutes or until mushrooms have darkened and all liquid has evaporated, stirring occasionally. Add 2¾ cups broth; bring to a boil. Reduce heat to medium-low and simmer, uncovered, 10 to 12 minutes or until broth is reduced by one-third. Return liquid to a boil.

Combine cornstarch and remaining ¼ cup broth in small cup. Add to mushroom mixture. Boil, stirring constantly, 1 to 2 minutes or until thickened. Stir in parsley, salt and pepper sauce.

Makes about 3 cups

Chunky Pasta Sauce with Meat

6 ounces ground beef
6 ounces mild or hot Italian sausage, sliced
½ medium onion, coarsely chopped
1 clove garlic, minced
2 cans (14½ ounces each) DEL MONTE® Diced Tomatoes with Basil, Garlic & Oregano
1 can (8 ounces) DEL MONTE® Tomato Sauce
¼ cup red wine (optional)
Hot cooked pasta
Grated Parmesan cheese

1. Brown beef and sausage in large saucepan; drain all but 1 tablespoon drippings.

2. Add onion and garlic; cook until tender.

3. Add undrained tomatoes, tomato sauce and wine. Boil, uncovered, 15 minutes, stirring frequently. Serve over pasta; top with Parmesan cheese.

Makes 4 servings (4 cups sauce)

Prep Time: 5 minutes   **Cook Time:** 25 minutes

Golden Sauce

½ pound (8 ounces) VELVEETA® Pasteurized Prepared Cheese Product, cut up
¼ cup milk

1. Stir Velveeta and milk in saucepan on low heat until smooth. Serve over hot cooked pasta or vegetables.

Makes 1 cup

Microwave Directions: Microwave Velveeta and milk in 1½-quart microwavable bowl on HIGH 2½ to 4½ minutes or until smooth, stirring every minute. Serve as directed.

Prep Time: 5 minutes   **Cook Time:** 10 minutes

Salsa Sauce

1¾ to 2 pounds fresh plum tomatoes, finely chopped
⅔ cup finely chopped fresh cilantro
½ cup finely chopped onion
2 jalapeño peppers,* seeded and minced
2 cloves garlic, minced
3 tablespoons lime juice
¼ teaspoon salt
½ cup shredded sharp provolone cheese
    Pasta, cooked and drained

Jalapeño peppers can sting and irritate the skin; wear rubber gloves when handling peppers and do not touch eyes. Wash hands after handling peppers.

1. Combine tomatoes, cilantro, onion, jalapeño, garlic, lime juice and salt in large bowl; set aside ½ hour to allow flavors to blend.

2. Place half of tomato mixture in food processor or blender; process until smooth. Return to bowl with remaining tomato mixture; stir together. To serve, place sauce over hot pasta and sprinkle cheese over top.   *Makes 8 (½-cup) servings*

Tomato-Eggplant Sauce

    Olive oil-flavored nonstick cooking spray
1 small eggplant, coarsely chopped
½ cup chopped onion
2 cloves garlic, minced
½ teaspoon dried tarragon leaves
¼ teaspoon dried thyme leaves
1 can (16 ounces) no-salt-added whole tomatoes, undrained and coarsely
    chopped
    Salt and black pepper

1. Spray large skillet with cooking spray; heat over medium heat until hot. Add eggplant, onion, garlic, tarragon and thyme; cook and stir about 5 minutes or until vegetables are tender.

2. Stir in tomatoes with juice; bring to a boil. Reduce heat and simmer, uncovered, 3 to 4 minutes. Season to taste with salt and pepper.   *Makes about 2½ cups*

Creamy Roasted Red Pepper Sauce

1½ to 2 pounds red bell peppers (about 3 bell peppers)
3 tablespoons plain nonfat yogurt
2 tablespoons grated Parmesan cheese
1 tablespoon chopped fresh parsley
2 cloves garlic
⅛ teaspoon salt

1. Preheat oven to 500°F. Place peppers on bottom oven rack. Cook, turning occasionally, until all sides are charred and peppers are soft. Remove from oven; place in brown bag to cool (this makes peeling the skin easier). Remove skins and seeds.

2. Place peppers, yogurt, cheese, parsley, garlic and salt in food processor or blender; process 1 minute or until small pieces of pepper remain. Top over short cut pasta. *Makes 6 (¼-cup) servings*

Hunt's® Spaghetti Sauce

½ pound ground beef
¼ cup chopped onion
2 (8-ounce) cans HUNT'S® Tomato Sauce
¾ teaspoon sugar
½ teaspoon dried basil leaves
¼ teaspoon dried oregano leaves
¼ teaspoon garlic powder

Brown beef with onion in medium saucepan over medium-high heat until no longer pink; drain. Stir in tomato sauce, sugar, basil, oregano and garlic powder. Simmer, covered, 10 minutes; stir occasionally. *Makes 2 cups*

Neopolitan Sauce

½ cup minced green bell pepper
¼ cup minced onion
¼ cup coarsely chopped celery
 2 cloves garlic, minced
 1 teaspoon olive oil
 2 cans (10 ounces each) no-salt-added whole tomatoes, undrained
¼ cup chopped fresh parsley
 1 tablespoon chopped fresh basil
¼ teaspoon salt
⅛ teaspoon black pepper
    Pasta, cooked and drained

1. Place bell pepper, onion, celery, garlic and oil in medium saucepan. Cook and stir over medium heat until onion is tender.

2. Add tomatoes, parsley, basil, salt and black pepper. Reduce heat to low; cover. Simmer 15 minutes; uncover. Cook and stir 10 minutes or until sauce thickens. Serve over pasta.   *Makes 8 (½-cup) servings*

Gorgonzola Sauce

 3 tablespoons butter or margarine
¼ cup all-purpose flour
 2 cups milk
¼ cup canned vegetable broth
½ teaspoon black pepper
 4 ounces Gorgonzola, crumbled

1. Melt butter in small saucepan over medium heat. Stir in flour. Cook and stir 2 to 3 minutes or until bubbly. Gradually stir in milk, broth and pepper. Cook until thickened, stirring constantly.

2. Reduce heat to low. Stir in cheese until melted.   *Makes about 2½ cups*

Olive-Basil Pesto Sauce

.1 cup kalamata olives, divided
1 cup packed fresh basil
¾ cup pine nuts or walnuts, toasted*
1 clove garlic
½ cup Parmesan cheese
½ cup olive oil
2 tablespoons chopped pimiento

To toast nuts, spread them in a single layer on baking sheet. Bake in preheated 350°F oven 8 to 10 minutes or until brown, stirring twice.

1. Rinse olives and pat dry with paper towels. Using small utility knife, slit open each olive and remove pit. Reserve ¼ cup olives.

2. Combine basil, ¾ cup olives, pine nuts and garlic in food processor or blender container; process until smooth. Add cheese. With machine running, pour oil through feed tube, processing until ingredients are well blended. Coarsely chop reserved ¼ cup olives. Stir olives and pimiento into mixture. Serve at room temperature. *Makes about 1½ cups*

Note: Pesto may be stored in refrigerator up to 2 weeks or frozen up to 3 months. Cover top of pesto with thin layer of olive oil before storing.

Parmesan White Sauce

4 tablespoons margarine
¼ cup plus 3 tablespoons all-purpose flour
1 can (14½ ounces) fat-free reduced-sodium chicken broth
2⅔ cups fat-free (skim) milk
⅓ cup grated Parmesan cheese
2 teaspoons dried oregano leaves
1½ teaspoons dried sage leaves
¼ teaspoon ground nutmeg
Salt and black pepper

Melt margarine in large saucepan over medium heat. Stir in flour; cook and stir 1 to 2 minutes. Whisk in chicken broth and milk; bring to a boil. Boil, whisking constantly, 1 to 2 minutes or until thickened. Remove from heat; stir in cheese, oregano, sage and nutmeg. Season to taste with salt and pepper.
Makes about 4⅔ cups (8 servings)

Favorite recipe: _____

Favorite recipe from: _____

Ingredients: _____

_____

_____

_____

_____

_____

Method: _____

_____

_____

_____

_____

_____

_____

_____

_____

_____

Favorite recipe: _____

Favorite recipe from: _____

Ingredients: _____

_____

_____

_____

_____

_____

Method: _____

_____

_____

_____

_____

_____

_____

_____

_____

_____

_____

Favorite recipe: _____

Favorite recipe from: _____

Ingredients: _____

_____

_____

_____

_____

_____

_____

Method: _____

_____

_____

_____

_____

_____

_____

_____

_____

_____

_____

Favorite recipe: _____

Favorite recipe from: _____

Ingredients: _____

_____

_____

_____

_____

_____

Method: _____

_____

_____

_____

_____

_____

_____

_____

_____

_____

Favorite recipe: _____

Favorite recipe from: _____

Ingredients: _____

_____

_____

_____

_____

_____

Method: _____

_____

_____

_____

_____

_____

_____

_____

_____

_____

_____

_____

Favorite recipe: _____

Favorite recipe from: _____

Ingredients: _____

_____

_____

_____

_____

_____

Method: _____

_____

_____

_____

_____

_____

_____

_____

_____

_____

_____

Favorite recipe: _____

Favorite recipe from: _____

Ingredients: _____

_____

_____

_____

_____

_____

_____

Method: _____

_____

_____

_____

_____

_____

_____

_____

_____

_____

_____

Favorite recipe: _____

Favorite recipe from: _____

Ingredients: _____

_____

_____

_____

_____

_____

Method: _____

_____

_____

_____

_____

_____

_____

_____

_____

_____

_____

Favorite recipe: _____

Favorite recipe from: _____

Ingredients: _____

_____

_____

_____

_____

Method: _____

_____

_____

_____

_____

_____

_____

_____

_____

_____

Favorite recipe: _____

Favorite recipe from: _____

Ingredients: _____

_____

_____

_____

_____

_____

Method: _____

_____

_____

_____

_____

_____

_____

_____

_____

_____

_____

Favorite recipe: _____

Favorite recipe from: _____

Ingredients: _____

_____

_____

_____

_____

_____

Method: _____

_____

_____

_____

_____

_____

_____

_____

_____

_____

Favorite recipe: _____

Favorite recipe from: _____

Ingredients: _____

_____

_____

_____

_____

_____

Method: _____

_____

_____

_____

_____

_____

_____

_____

_____

_____

Favorite recipe: _____

Favorite recipe from: _____

Ingredients: _____

_____

_____

_____

_____

_____

Method: _____

_____

_____

_____

_____

_____

_____

_____

_____

_____

_____

_____

Favorite recipe: _____

Favorite recipe from: _____

Ingredients: _____

_____

_____

_____

_____

_____

Method: _____

_____

_____

_____

_____

_____

_____

_____

_____

_____

_____

Favorite recipe: _____

Favorite recipe from: _____

Ingredients: _____

_____

_____

_____

_____

_____

Method: _____

_____

_____

_____

_____

_____

_____

_____

_____

_____

_____

_____

Favorite recipe: _____

Favorite recipe from: _____

Ingredients: _____

_____

_____

_____

_____

_____

Method: _____

_____

_____

_____

_____

_____

_____

_____

_____

_____

Favorite recipe: _____

Favorite recipe from: _____

Ingredients: _____

_____

_____

_____

_____

_____

Method: _____

_____

_____

_____

_____

_____

_____

_____

_____

_____

_____

Favorite recipe: _____

Favorite recipe from: _____

Ingredients: _____

_____

_____

_____

_____

_____

Method: _____

_____

_____

_____

_____

_____

_____

_____

_____

_____

_____

Favorite recipe: _____

Favorite recipe from: _____

Ingredients: _____

_____

_____

_____

_____

_____

Method: _____

_____

_____

_____

_____

_____

_____

_____

_____

_____

_____

Favorite recipe: _____

Favorite recipe from: _____

Ingredients: _____

_____

_____

_____

_____

_____

Method: _____

_____

_____

_____

_____

_____

_____

_____

_____

_____

_____

_____

Favorite recipe: _____

Favorite recipe from: _____

Ingredients: _____

_____

_____

_____

_____

_____

Method: _____

_____

_____

_____

_____

_____

_____

_____

_____

_____

_____

Favorite recipe: _____

Favorite recipe from: _____

Ingredients: _____

_____

_____

_____

_____

_____

Method: _____

_____

_____

_____

_____

_____

_____

_____

_____

_____

_____

_____

Favorite recipe: _____

Favorite recipe from: _____

Ingredients: _____

_____

_____

_____

_____

_____

Method: _____

_____

_____

_____

_____

_____

_____

_____

_____

_____

Favorite recipe: _____

Favorite recipe from: _____

Ingredients: _____

_____

_____

_____

_____

_____

Method: _____

_____

_____

_____

_____

_____

_____

_____

_____

_____

_____

_____

_____

Favorite recipe: _____

Favorite recipe from: _____

Ingredients: _____

_____

_____

_____

_____

_____

Method: _____

_____

_____

_____

_____

_____

_____

_____

_____

_____

_____

Favorite recipe: _____

Favorite recipe from: _____

Ingredients: _____

_____

_____

_____

_____

_____

Method: _____

_____

_____

_____

_____

_____

_____

_____

_____

_____

_____

_____

Favorite recipe: _____

Favorite recipe from: _____

Ingredients: _____

_____

_____

_____

_____

_____

Method: _____

_____

_____

_____

_____

_____

_____

_____

_____

_____

_____

_____

Favorite recipe: _____

Favorite recipe from: _____

Ingredients: _____

_____

_____

_____

_____

_____

Method: _____

_____

_____

_____

_____

_____

_____

_____

_____

_____

_____

Favorite recipe: _____

Favorite recipe from: _____

Ingredients: _____

_____

_____

_____

_____

_____

Method: _____

_____

_____

_____

_____

_____

_____

_____

_____

_____

_____

Favorite recipe: _____

Favorite recipe from: _____

Ingredients: _____

_____

_____

_____

_____

Method: _____

_____

_____

_____

_____

_____

_____

_____

_____

_____

_____

Favorite recipe: _____

Favorite recipe from: _____

Ingredients: _____

_____

_____

_____

_____

_____

_____

Method: _____

_____

_____

_____

_____

_____

_____

_____

_____

_____

_____

_____

_____

Favorite recipe: _____

Favorite recipe from: _____

Ingredients: _____

_____

_____

_____

_____

_____

Method: _____

_____

_____

_____

_____

_____

_____

_____

_____

_____

_____

_____

Bread crumbs	1 slice fresh bread = ½ cup coarse crumbs 8-ounce package = 2¼ cups
Cheddar cheese	¼ pound = 1 cup grated
Chicken	2 whole breasts = about 2 cups chopped cooked chicken
Chicken broth	13¾-ounce can = 1¾ cups
Coconut	4-ounce bag = 1⅔ cups
Cucumber	1 medium = 1½ cups sliced
Garlic	2 medium cloves = 1 teaspoon minced
Herbs	1 tablespoon fresh = 1 teaspoon dried
Nut meats	4 ounces = ¾ cup chopped
Onions, yellow	1 medium = ½ to ¾ cup chopped
Parmesan cheese	¼ pound = 1 cup grated
Peas	10-ounce package frozen = 2 cups
Peppers, bell	1 large = 1 cup chopped
Rice, long-grain white	1 cup = 3 cups cooked
Rice, brown	1 cup = 3 to 4 cups cooked
Shrimp	1 pound = 10 to 15 jumbo 1 pound = 16 to 20 large 1 pound = 25 to 30 medium
Sour cream	8 ounces = 1 cup
Tomatoes	1 pound (3 medium) = 1½ cups peeled and drained

BUYING TIPS

- Inspect the chicken before purchasing. The skin should be creamy white to deep yellow. The chicken should be plump, and the meat should never look gray or pasty.

- Look for secure, unbroken packaging, as well as a "sell-by" date that indicates the last day the chicken should be sold.

- Two whole chicken breasts yield about two cups chopped cooked chicken; one broiler-fryer (about three pounds) yields about two and one-half cups chopped cooked chicken.

STORING TIPS

- Raw chicken is very perishable and must be handled with care. Buy it just before returning home, and refrigerate it as soon as possible.

- Fresh raw chicken can be stored in its original packaging for up to two days in the coldest part of the refrigerator.

- Freeze chicken immediately if you do not plan to use it within two days after purchasing. You can freeze raw chicken, tightly wrapped in plastic wrap, freezer paper or foil, for up to one year.

- Cooked chicken can be frozen for up to two months.

Raw chicken can contain salmonella bacteria, but with careful handling and proper cooking methods you can eliminate any health concerns. Follow these helpful tips for safe handling of chicken:

- **Do not** thaw frozen chicken on the kitchen counter, because bacteria grow more quickly at room temperature. Instead, thaw wrapped chicken in the refrigerator.

- Allow at least 24 hours thawing time for a 5-pound whole chicken. Allow five hours thawing time per pound of chicken pieces.

- **Do not** allow other food to come in contact with a thawing chicken or its juices.

- Raw chicken should be rinsed and patted dry with paper towels before cooking.

- Wash your hands thoroughly before and after handling raw chicken.

- Cutting boards and knives must be washed in hot, sudsy water after being used to cut raw chicken and before being used for any other food preparation.

- Never refreeze chicken that has been thawed.

- Chicken should be eaten, refrigerated or frozen within two hours of cooking.

- Always cook chicken completely. **Do not** partially cook, then store it to be finished cooking later.

- When stuffing chicken, lightly stuff the cavity just before cooking. **Do not** stuff chicken ahead of time.

Quick Tips

- Save food preparation time by purchasing precut vegetables, precooked meats, precut shredded cheeses and prechopped garlic.

- Kitchen scissors are the perfect tool to use for slicing a green onion fast.

- Keep a bottle of Italian salad dressing on hand for a quick way to add zesty flavor to sandwiches. It's also the perfect ready-made marinade for meats and poultry.

- Seed and chop sweet bell peppers and store them in a freezer bag in your freezer. They will be ready to use when you are making a dish in a hurry.

- Ripen a tomato faster by placing it in a paper bag along with an apple.

- Cut up canned tomatoes quickly by using kitchen shears to snip the tomatoes right in the can.

- Make out a weekly meal plan and prepare a shopping list. Do all your shopping at once instead of making nightly visits to the grocery store on your way home from work.

- When preparing a meal, make enough for leftovers for another meal of the week.

- Keep your pantry well-stocked with your favorite staples, and you'll have great dinner ideas ready at your fingertips.

- Weekends are the perfect time to prepare dishes you can heat up during the week when you're short of time.

- Wait until the cooking water boils before adding salt, since salted water takes longer to boil than unsalted water.

- Plan on preparing an extra batch of your favorite pasta soup or sauce. Pour it into serving-size freezer containers and freeze. Thaw and reheat for a last-minute dinner or quick lunch.

- Lasagna, manicotti and stuffed shells are perfect dishes to prepare and freeze for another time. Try freezing casseroles in single-serving portions for days when quick meals are necessary. Heat to serving temperature in the microwave or conventional oven.

- When cooking pasta, add extra to the boiling water so you will have leftovers. If you like, toss the leftover pasta with a little olive oil to help prevent sticking.

- Use plain leftover pasta as a base or extender for salads, soups, side dishes and casseroles. Simply store the leftover pasta in a plastic bag in the refrigerator for up to 3 days. Freshen the pasta by rinsing with hot or cold water, depending on how you plan to use it. Pasta can also be frozen and then reheated in boiling water or microwaved for a fresh cooked texture and taste. Make an easy and refreshing salad by tossing leftover spaghetti with diced raw vegetables and Italian salad dressing.

- Combine leftover cooked meats, poultry, fish and vegetables with your favorite pasta shape and a simple sauce for a fast new meal.

Use this chart as a simple guide to ingredient amounts and cooking times for cooking pasta.

Dried Pasta	Amount	Water	Boiling Time	Yield
Angel Hair	4 ounces	4 quarts	5 to 7 minutes	2 cups
Bow Ties	2 cups	4 quarts	10 minutes	2½ cups
Elbow Macaroni	2 cups	4 quarts	10 minutes	3 cups
Fettuccine	4 ounces	4 quarts	8 to 10 minutes	2 cups
Orzo	2 cups	4 quarts	5 to 8 minutes	4 cups
Spaghetti	4 ounces	4 quarts	10 to 12 minutes	2 cups

Dry Pasta: Store dry uncooked pasta in a cool, dry place. One cup of uncooked macaroni-type pasta will yield 2 cups cooked pasta. For every pound of dry pasta, bring 4 to 6 quarts of water to a full, rolling boil. Add 2 teaspoons salt, if desired. Gradually add pasta, allowing water to return to a boil. The water helps circulate the pasta so that it cooks evenly. Stir frequently to prevent the pasta from sticking. Begin testing for doneness at the minimum recommended time given on the package directions. Pasta should be "al dente"—tender, yet firm, not mushy. Immediately drain pasta to prevent overcooking. For best results, toss the pasta with sauce immediately after draining. If the sauce is not ready, toss the pasta with some butter or oil to prevent it from sticking.

Fresh Pasta: Homemade pasta takes less time to cook than dry pasta. Cook fresh pasta in the same manner as dry, except begin testing for doneness after 2 minutes. Fresh pasta will last several weeks in the refrigerator, or it can be frozen for up to 1 month.

Is It Done Yet?

Use the following guides to test for doneness.

CASSEROLES

until hot and bubbly

until heated through

until cheese melts

MEAT

Beef

medium 140°F to 145°F

well done 160°F

Veal

medium 145°F to 150°F

well done 160°F

Lamb

medium 145°F

well done 160°F

Pork

well done 165°F to 170°F

POULTRY

Chicken

until temperature in thigh is 180°F (whole bird)

until chicken is no longer pink in center

until temperature in breast is 170°F

SEAFOOD

Fish

until fish begins to flake against the grain when tested with fork

Shrimp

until shrimp are pink and opaque

SAUCES

until (slightly) thickened

SOUPS

until heated through

STEWS

until meat is tender

until vegetables are tender

VEGETABLES

until crisp-tender

until tender

until browned

Metric Conversion Chart

VOLUME MEASUREMENTS (dry)

$\frac{1}{8}$ teaspoon = 0.5 mL
$\frac{1}{4}$ teaspoon = 1 mL
$\frac{1}{2}$ teaspoon = 2 mL
$\frac{3}{4}$ teaspoon = 4 mL
1 teaspoon = 5 mL
1 tablespoon = 15 mL
2 tablespoons = 30 mL
$\frac{1}{4}$ cup = 60 mL
$\frac{1}{3}$ cup = 75 mL
$\frac{1}{2}$ cup = 125 mL
$\frac{2}{3}$ cup = 150 mL
$\frac{3}{4}$ cup = 175 mL
1 cup = 250 mL
2 cups = 1 pint = 500 mL
3 cups = 750 mL
4 cups = 1 quart = 1 L

VOLUME MEASUREMENTS (fluid)

1 fluid ounce (2 tablespoons) = 30 mL
4 fluid ounces ($\frac{1}{2}$ cup) = 125 mL
8 fluid ounces (1 cup) = 250 mL
12 fluid ounces (1$\frac{1}{2}$ cups) = 375 mL
16 fluid ounces (2 cups) = 500 mL

WEIGHTS (mass)

$\frac{1}{2}$ ounce = 15 g
1 ounce = 30 g
3 ounces = 90 g
4 ounces = 120 g
8 ounces = 225 g
10 ounces = 285 g
12 ounces = 360 g
16 ounces = 1 pound = 450 g

DIMENSIONS

$\frac{1}{16}$ inch = 2 mm
$\frac{1}{8}$ inch = 3 mm
$\frac{1}{4}$ inch = 6 mm
$\frac{1}{2}$ inch = 1.5 cm
$\frac{3}{4}$ inch = 2 cm
1 inch = 2.5 cm

OVEN TEMPERATURES

250°F = 120°C
275°F = 140°C
300°F = 150°C
325°F = 160°C
350°F = 180°C
375°F = 190°C
400°F = 200°C
425°F = 220°C
450°F = 230°C

BAKING PAN SIZES

Utensil	Size in Inches/Quarts	Metric Volume	Size in Centimeters
Baking or Cake Pan (square or rectangular)	8×8×2	2 L	20×20×5
	9×9×2	2.5 L	23×23×5
	12×8×2	3 L	30×20×5
	13×9×2	3.5 L	33×23×5
Loaf Pan	8×4×3	1.5 L	20×10×7
	9×5×3	2 L	23×13×7
Round Layer Cake Pan	8×1½	1.2 L	20×4
	9×1½	1.5 L	23×4
Pie Plate	8×1¼	750 mL	20×3
	9×1¼	1 L	23×3
Baking Dish or Casserole	1 quart	1 L	—
	1½ quart	1.5 L	—
	2 quart	2 L	—

Acknowledgments

The publisher would like to thank the companies and organizations listed below for the use of their recipes and photographs in this publication.

A.1.® Steak Sauce

Barilla America, Inc.

BelGioioso® Cheese, Inc.

Birds Eye®

Butterball® Turkey Company

Colorado Potato Administrative Committee

ConAgra Grocery Products Company

Delmarva Poultry Industry, Inc.

Del Monte Corporation

Dole Food Company, Inc.

Filippo Berio® Olive Oil

Florida Tomato Committee

The Fremont Company, Makers of Frank's & SnowFloss Kraut and Tomato Products

The Golden Grain Company®

Hillshire Farm®

Holland House® is a registered trademark of Mott's, Inc.

Hormel Foods, LLC

The HV Company

Kahlúa® Liqueur

Kikkoman International Inc.

The Kingsford Products Company

Kraft Foods Holdings

Lawry's® Foods, Inc.

Lipton®

McIlhenny Company (TABASCO® brand Pepper Sauce)

National Chicken Council

Nestlé USA

Newman's Own, Inc.

Norseland, Inc.

North Dakota Beef Commission

North Dakota Wheat Commission

Perdue Farms Incorporated

The Procter & Gamble Company

The Quaker® Oatmeal Kitchens

Reckitt Benckiser

RED STAR® Yeast, a product of Lasaffre Yeast Corporation

Riviana Foods Inc.

Sargento® Foods Inc.

Sonoma® Dried Tomatoes

The Sugar Association, Inc.

Sunkist Growers

Uncle Ben's Inc.

Unilever Bestfoods North America

USA Dry Pea & Lentil Council

USA Rice Federation

Veg-All®

Walnut Marketing Board

Washington Apple Commission

Wisconsin Milk Marketing Board

Recipe Index

A

Albóndigas Soup, 128
All-in-One Burger Stew, 142
Almond Chicken Cups, 12
Almond Chicken Kabobs, 14
Antipasto Salad, 192
Apples
  Chicken Curry Soup, 25
  Crunchy Apple Salsa with Grilled
    Chicken, 74
  Grilled Chicken and Apple with Fresh
    Rosemary, 70
  Pasta Waldorf, 220
  Pennsylvania Dutch Chicken Bake, 47
Artichoke Casserole, 104
Asian Chicken and Noodles, 52
Asian Pesto, 63
Asian Spaghetti, 212

B

Bacon
  Bacon & Cheese Stuffed Chicken, 44
  BLT Chicken Salad for Two, 26
  Cobb Salad with Tarragon Dressing,
    26
  Southern-Style Chicken and Greens,
    42
Baked Barbecue Chicken, 38
Baked Chicken with Crispy Cheese-
    Garlic Crust, 41
Balsamic Chicken Salad, 32
Barbecue Sauce, 16
Basil Shrimp Fettuccine, 204
Beans
  Beefy Bean & Walnut Stir-Fry, 158
  Black Bean and Mango Chicken Salad,
    28
  Crunchy Layered Beef & Bean Salad,
    146
  Durango Chili, 134
  Fast 'n' Easy Chili, 148
  Five-Way Cincinnati Chili, 164
  Mango & Black Bean Salsa, 66
  Meaty Chili, 141
  Mexican Vegetable Beef Soup, 130
  Minute Minestrone Soup, 174
  Monterey Black Bean Tortilla Supper,
    108
  Noodly Chicken & Green Bean Skillet,
    38
  Pantry Soup, 25, 170
  Pasta e Fagioli, 176
  Pasta Fazool, 205
  Peppery Grilled Salad, 71

Beans *(continued)*
  Quick & Easy Chili, 132
  Ranch Lentil Casserole, 106
  Rapid Ragú® Chili, 138
  Riverboat Chili, 142
  Speedy Beef & Bean Burrito, 154
  Spicy Quick and Easy Chili, 135
  Taco Pot Pie, 124
  Tamale Pie, 110
  Tex-Mex Beef & Black Bean Skillet,
    122
  30-Minute Chili Mac, 202
Beef *(see also pages 82–160)*
  Beef Stroganoff, 198
  Cheesy Skillet Lasagna, 202
  Chunky Pasta Sauce with Meat, 232
  Five-Way Cincinnati Chili, 164
  Hunts® Spaghetti Sauce, 236
  Oriental Steak Salad, 190
  Quick Beef Soup, 166
  30-Minute Chili Mac, 202
Beefy Bean & Walnut Stir-Fry, 158
Beefy Nacho Crescent Bake, 96
Big Easy Chicken Creole, 36
Bistro Burgers with Blue Cheese, 154
Bite Size Tacos, 156
Black Bean and Mango Chicken Salad,
    28
BLT Chicken Salad for Two, 26
Blue Cheese Chicken Salad, 30
Broccoli
  Broccoli and Beef Pasta, 126
  Broccoli Shrimp Pasta, 196
  Chicken Walnut Stir-Fry, 64
  Lime-Mustard Marinated Chicken, 70
Buffalo Bar-B-Q Nuggets, 4
Buffalo Chicken Wings, 8

C

Caesar Shrimp Pasta Salad, 188
California Chef Salad, 32
California Tamale Pie, 98
Carrots
  Albóndigas Soup, 128
  Chicken Salad with Goat Cheese, 31
  Classic Meatball Soup, 136
  Couscous with Vegetables in Savory
    Broth, 224
  Garden Vegetable Linguine, 206
  Pasta Fazool, 205
  Pasta Primavera, 214
  Salsa Corn Soup with Chicken, 22
  Szechwan Beef, 121
  White Cheddar Seafood Chowder, 171

Recipe Index

Casseroles (*see also pages 96–113*)
Easy Mostaccioli Casserole, 84
Swiss 'n' Chicken Casserole, 46
Cheeseburger Macaroni, 120
Cheesy Shells, 224
Cheesy Skillet Lasagna, 202
Chicken (*see also pages 2–80*)
Chicken and Fruit Kabobs, 71
Chicken Burritos, 59
Chicken Curry Soup, 25
Chicken di Napolitano, 62
Chicken Marsala, 60
Chicken Rotini Soup, 172
Chicken Salad, 31
Chicken Salad with Goat Cheese, 31
Chicken Shish-Kebabs, 74
Chicken Tortellini Soup, 171
Chicken Vesuvio, 54
Chicken Walnut Stir-Fry, 64
Chicken with Brandied Fruit Sauce, 47
Chicken with Roasted Garlic
    Marinara, 63
Crispy Lemon Pepper Chicken with
    Spinach Pasta, 210
Dressed Chicken Breasts with Angel
    Hair Pasta, 200
Original Ranch® Tetrazzini, 205
Pantry Soup, 25, 170
Salsa Corn Soup with Chicken, 22
Tuscan Chicken and Pasta, 194
Tuscany Chicken Soup, 164
Chili
Chili Beef Mac, 136
Chili-Crusted Grilled Chicken Caesar
    Salad, 30
Durango Chili, 134
Fast 'n' Easy Chili, 148
Five-Way Cincinnati Chili, 164
Hearty Chili Mac, 130
Meaty Chili, 141
Quick & Easy Chili, 132
Ragú® Chili Mac, 116
Rapid Ragú® Chili, 138
Riverboat Chili, 142
Spicy Quick and Easy Chili, 135
Texas-Style Chili, 140
Chuckwagon BBQ Rice Round-Up, 114
Chunky Pasta Sauce with Meat, 232
Citrus Chicken, 54
Classic Chicken Biscuit Pie, 51
Classic Chicken Parmesan, 58
Classic Grilled Chicken, 77
Classic Meatball Soup, 136
Cobb Salad with Tarragon Dressing, 26

Coconut Chicken Tenders with Spicy
    Mango Salsa, 8
Cool Teriyaki Dipping Sauce, 14
Corn
Black Bean and Mango Chicken Salad,
    28
California Tamale Pie, 98
Chuckwagon BBQ Rice Round-Up,
    114
Corny Sloppy Joes, 156
Farmer's Stew Argentina, 140
Groovy Angel Hair Goulash, 152
Rocky Mountain Hash with Smoked
    Chicken, 40
Salsa Corn Soup with Chicken, 22
Southwestern Chicken Soup, 22
Southwestern Meat Loaf, 88
Spicy Quick and Easy Chili, 135
Szechwan Beef, 121
Taco Pot Pie, 124
Taco Salad, 186
Texas Beef Stew, 132
Tomato Chicken Gumbo, 24
Western Wagon Wheels, 124
Corny Sloppy Joes, 156
Country Chicken Pot Pie, 48
Country Chicken Stew, 20
Couscous with Vegetables in Savory
    Broth, 224
Creamy Beef and Vegetable Casserole,
    148
Creamy Cheddar Cheese Soup, 166
Creamy Herbed Chicken, 36
Creamy Pasta Primavera, 204
Creamy Roasted Red Pepper Sauce, 236
Creamy Vegetables & Pasta, 226
Crispy Lemon Pepper Chicken with
    Spinach Pasta, 210
Crunchy Apple Salsa with Grilled
    Chicken, 74
Crunchy Layered Beef & Bean Salad,
    146
Curried Buffalo Wings, 7
Curry Beef, 122

D
Deep Dish All-American Pizza, 84
Dressed Chicken Breasts with Angel
    Hair Pasta, 200
Durango Chili, 134

E
Easy Cheesy Pastina, 218
Easy Mostaccioli Casserole, 84

F

Family Barbecued Chicken, 76
Farmer's Stew Argentina, 140
Fast 'n' Easy Chili, 148
Favorite Macaroni Salad, 186
Fish (*see also* **Shellfish**)
  Italian Fish Soup, 176
  Tuna Mac, 196
Five-Way Cincinnati Chili, 164
Fresh 'n' Sassy Spaghetti Sauce, 228
Fresh Orange-Pasta Salad, 184

G

Garden Pasta Salad, 180
Garden Vegetable Linguine, 206
Garlicky Baked Chicken, 46
Garlicky Gilroy Chicken Wings, 10
Ginger Wings with Peach Dipping Sauce,
  18
Golden Sauce, 232
Gorgonzola Buffalo Wings, 18
Gorgonzola Sauce, 238
Greek Beef & Rice, 118
Greek-Style Lasagna, 110
Greens and Gemelli, 208
Grilled Chicken and Apple with Fresh
  Rosemary, 70
Grilled Chicken and Vegetable Kabobs,
  78
Grilled Chicken Croissant with Roasted
  Pepper Dressing, 80
Grilled Chicken with Asian Pesto, 63
Grilled Greek Chicken, 72
Grilled Italian Chicken, 56
Grilled Meat Loaves and Potatoes, 94
Grilled Vegetable and Chicken Pasta,
  78
Groovy Angel Hair Goulash, 152

H

Hanoi Beef and Rice Soup, 135
Heartland Shepherd's Pie, 112
Hearty Beef Stew, 134
Hearty Chili Mac, 130
Hidden Valley Fried Chicken, 50
Hidden Valley Ranch® Tortellini Salad,
  182
Honey Baked Chicken, 40
Honey Mustard BBQ Chicken Stir-Fry,
  51
Hot & Cool Teriyaki Wings, 14
Hot & Spicy Buffalo Chicken Wings, 2
Hot 'n' Spicy Chicken Barbecue, 68
Hunts® Spaghetti Sauce, 236

I

Italian Beef Burrito, 118
Italian Fish Soup, 176
Italian Pasta & Vegetable Salad, 188
Italian Pasta Bake, 198
Italian Vegetable Salad, 190

J

Jerk Chicken and Pasta, 56
Jerk Sauce, 56
Joe's Special, 116

K

Kahlúa® Stir-Fry Chicken, 41
Kung Pao Chicken, 58

L

Lasagna Beef 'n' Spinach Roll-Ups, 112
Lasagna Roll-Ups, 94
Lasagna Supreme, 92
Lime-Mustard Marinated Chicken, 70
Linguine with Oil and Garlic, 214
Lipton® Onion Burgers, 91
Long Soup, 172

M

Macaroni and Cheese Pronto, 206
Main-Dish Pie, 160
Malaysian Curried Beef, 100
Mandarin Orange Chicken, 64
Mango & Black Bean Salsa, 66
Mangoes
  Black Bean and Mango Chicken Salad,
    28
  Coconut Chicken Tenders with Spicy
    Mango Salsa, 8
  Mango & Black Bean Salsa, 66
  Spicy Mango Chicken, 66
Manicotti Parmigiana, 85
Meaty Chili, 141
Mediterranean Burgers, 88
Mediterranean Orzo Salad, 180
Mediterranean Orzo with Pesto,
  222
Mexican Stuffed Shells, 108
Mexican Vegetable Beef Soup, 130
Minestrone Soup with Mini Meatballs,
  138
Mini Meat Loaves & Vegetables, 91
Mini Mexican Burger Bites, 150
Mini Penne with Mascarpone, 226
Minute Minestrone Soup, 174
Monterey Black Bean Tortilla Supper,
  108

Mushrooms
Artichoke Casserole, 104
Beef Stroganoff Casserole, 98
Chicken Marsala, 60
Deep Dish All-American Pizza, 84
Grilled Chicken and Vegetable
Kabobs, 78
Joe's Special, 116
Kahlúa® Stir-Fry Chicken, 41
Lasagna Supreme, 92
Mushroom Chicken Rotini Soup, 172
Original Ranch® Tetrazzini, 205
Party Chicken Tarts, 6
Pasta Primavera, 214
Quick Beef Stroganoff, 126
Salisbury Steaks with Mushroom-Wine
Sauce, 144
Seafood Pasta, 210
Spinach-Potato Bake, 100
Sun-Dried Tomato Pesto, 230
Zesty Pasta Salad, 192

N
Nacho Bacho, 157
Neopolitan Sauce, 238
Noodly Chicken & Green Bean Skillet,
38
Nuts
Almond Chicken Cups, 12
Almond Chicken Kabobs, 14
Beefy Bean & Walnut Stir-Fry, 158
Chicken Walnut Stir-Fry, 64
Kahlúa® Stir-Fry Chicken, 41
Nutty Caesar Salad Pasta, 182
Nutty Oven-Fried Chicken
Drumsticks, 34
Olive-Basil Pesto Sauce, 240
Pasta Waldorf, 220
Pine Nut and Cilantro Pesto, 228
Tropical Chicken Salad, 28
Vegetable Almond Fettuccine, 208
Walnut Lemon Couscous, 220

O
Olive-Basil Pesto Sauce, 240
Olives
Antipasto Salad, 192
Easy Mostaccioli Casserole, 84
Garden Vegetable Linguine, 206
Mediterranean Orzo Salad, 180
Mediterranean Orzo with Pesto, 222
Nacho Bacho, 157
Olive-Basil Pesto Sauce, 240
Pepperoni Pasta Salad, 178

Olives *(continued)*
Quick Greek Pitas, 121
Sicilian-Style Pasta Salad, 184
Spaghetti with Fresh Tomato Sauce,
200
Walnut Lemon Couscous, 220
Onion Soup with Pasta, 174
Oriental Noodles, 216
Oriental Steak Salad, 190
Original Ranch® Tetrazzini, 205

P
Pantry Soup, 25, 170
Parmesan White Sauce, 240
Party Chicken Sandwiches, 16
Party Chicken Tarts, 6
Pasta *(see also pages 162–240)*
All-in-One Burger Stew, 142
Asian Chicken and Noodles, 52
Bacon & Cheese Stuffed Chicken, 44
Beef Stroganoff Casserole, 98
Broccoli and Beef Pasta, 126
Cheeseburger Macaroni, 120
Chicken Curry Soup, 25
Chicken Marsala, 60
Chicken with Roasted Garlic
Marinara, 63
Chili Beef Mac, 136
Classic Meatball Soup, 136
Creamy Herbed Chicken, 36
Curry Beef, 122
Easy Mostaccioli Casserole, 84
Grilled Vegetable and Chicken Pasta,
78
Groovy Angel Hair Goulash, 152
Hearty Chili Mac, 130
Honey Mustard BBQ Chicken Stir-Fry,
51
Jerk Chicken and Pasta, 56
Lasagna Beef 'n' Spinach Roll-Ups, 112
Lasagna Roll-Ups, 94
Lasagna Supreme, 92
Manicotti Parmigiana, 85
Mexican Stuffed Shells, 108
Noodly Chicken & Green Bean Skillet,
38
Pantry Soup, 25, 170
Pasta Beef & Zucchini Dinner, 120
Pasta e Fagioli, 176
Pasta Fazool, 205
Pasta Pesto Salad, 178
Pasta "Pizza," 101
Pasta Primavera, 214
Pasta Waldorf, 220

Recipe Index

Pasta *(continued)*
  Pasta with Zesty Tomato Pesto, 218
  Quick Beef Stroganoff, 126
  Ragú® Chili Mac, 116
  String Pie, 106
  Tacos in Pasta Shells, 102
  Vegetable Almond Fettuccine, 208
  Western Wagon Wheels, 124
  Zucchini Lasagne, 101
Peach Dipping Sauce, 18
Pennsylvania Dutch Chicken Bake,
  47
Pepper Glazed Cajun Chicken, 48
Pepperoni Pasta Salad, 178, 216
Peppers, Bell
  Almond Chicken Cups, 12
  Antipasto Salad, 192
  Big Easy Chicken Creole, 36
  Black Bean and Mango Chicken Salad,
  28
  Chicken Salad with Goat Cheese,
  31
  Chicken Shish-Kebabs, 74
  Chili Beef Mac, 136
  Coconut Chicken Tenders with Spicy
  Mango Salsa, 8
  Couscous with Vegetables in Savory
  Broth, 224
  Creamy Herbed Chicken, 36
  Creamy Roasted Red Pepper Sauce,
  236
  Deep Dish All-American Pizza, 84
  Durango Chili, 134
  Farmer's Stew Argentina, 140
  Garden Vegetable Linguine, 206
  Grilled Chicken and Vegetable
  Kabobs, 78
  Grilled Vegetable and Chicken Pasta,
  78
  Honey Mustard BBQ Chicken Stir-Fry,
  51
  Italian Beef Burrito, 118
  Italian Vegetable Salad, 190
  Jerk Chicken and Pasta, 56
  Kahlúa® Stir-Fry Chicken, 41
  Mediterranean Orzo Salad, 180
  Mini Mexican Burger Bites, 150
  Neopolitan Sauce, 238
  Oriental Noodles, 216
  Pasta Pesto Salad, 178
  Pasta "Pizza," 101
  Pepperoni Pasta Salad, 178
  Pizza Meat Loaf, 82
  Polynesian Burgers, 86

Peppers, Bell *(continued)*
  Quick 'n' Easy Tacos, 149
  Rice-Stuffed Peppers, 160
  Riverboat Chili, 142
  Roasted Tomato and Mozzarella Pasta
  Salad, 191
  Rocky Mountain Hash with Smoked
  Chicken, 40
  Saucy Stuffed Peppers, 90
  Sicilian-Style Pasta Salad, 184
  Sloppy Joe Rollers, 149
  Southwestern Meat Loaf, 88
  Stuffed Mexican Pizza Pie, 109
  Tempting Taco Burgers, 90
  Texas-Style Chili, 140
  Tomato Chicken Gumbo, 24
  Western Hash, 157
  Zesty Pasta Salad, 192
Peppery Grilled Salad, 71
Pesto & Tortellini Soup, 170
Pesto Chicken Brushetta, 12
Pine Nut and Cilantro Pesto, 228
Pizza Meat Loaf, 82
Polynesian Burgers, 86
Polynesian Chicken and Rice, 59
Pork Long Soup, 172
Potatoes
  Albóndigas Soup, 128
  Chicken Vesuvio, 54
  Country Chicken Stew, 20
  Grilled Meat Loaves and Potatoes, 94
  Heartland Shepherd's Pie, 112
  Hearty Beef Stew, 134
  Malaysian Curried Beef, 100
  Mini Meat Loaves & Vegetables, 91
  Rocky Mountain Hash with Smoked
  Chicken, 40
  Shepherd's Pie, 104
  Southwestern Chicken Soup, 22
  Spinach-Potato Bake, 100
  Taco Taters, 150
  Texas Beef Stew, 132
Primavera Tortellini en Brodo, 168

Q
Quick & Easy Chili, 132
Quick 'n' Easy Tacos, 149
Quick Beef Soup, 166
Quick Beef Stroganoff, 126
Quick Greek Pitas, 121

R
Ragú® Chili Mac, 116
Ranch Buffalo Wings, 7

Ranch Lentil Casserole, 106
Rapid Ragú® Chili, 138
Red Hot Pepper Wings, 7
Rice
  Albóndigas Soup, 128
  Chicken di Napolitano, 62
  Chicken Shish-Kebabs, 74
  Chuckwagon BBQ Rice Round-Up, 114
  Classic Chicken Biscuit Pie, 51
  Farmer's Stew Argentina, 140
  Greek Beef & Rice, 118
  Grilled Chicken and Vegetable Kabobs, 78
  Hanoi Beef and Rice Soup, 135
  Kung Pao Chicken, 58
  Polynesian Chicken and Rice, 59
  Rice-Stuffed Peppers, 160
  Simple Stir-Fry, 60
  Southern-Style Chicken and Greens, 42
  Spanish Skillet Supper, 62
  Special Occasion Meat Loaf, 85
  Stuffed Mexican Pizza Pie, 109
  Szechwan Beef, 121
  Tex-Mex Beef & Black Bean Skillet, 122
  Tomato Chicken Gumbo, 24
  Western Hash, 157
  Wild Rice Soup, 141
Riverboat Chili, 142
Roasted Fresh Tomatoes, 191
Roasted Tomato and Mozzarella Pasta Salad, 191
Rocky Mountain Hash with Smoked Chicken, 40

S
Salad Vinaigrette, 31
Salisbury Steaks with Mushroom-Wine Sauce, 144
Salsa Corn Soup with Chicken, 22
Salsa Sauce, 234
San Francisco Grilled Chicken, 80
Santa Fe Grilled Chicken, 76
Sauces *(see also pages 228–240)*
  Barbecue Sauce, 16
  Cool Teriyaki Dipping Sauce, 14
  Jerk Sauce, 56
  Peach Dipping Sauce, 18
Saucy Stuffed Peppers, 90
Sausage
  Chunky Pasta Sauce with Meat, 232
  Garden Vegetable Linguine, 206

Sausage *(continued)*
  Greens and Gemelli, 208
  Lasagna Supreme, 92
  Special Occasion Meat Loaf, 85
  Tomato Chicken Gumbo, 24
Seafood Pasta, 210
Sesame Chicken Nuggets, 16
Shellfish
  Basil Shrimp Fettuccine, 204
  Broccoli Shrimp Pasta, 196
  Caesar Shrimp Pasta Salad, 188
  Seafood Pasta, 210
  Sicilian-Style Pasta Salad, 184
Shepherd's Pie, 104
Sicilian-Style Pasta Salad, 184
Simple Stir-Fry, 60
Skillet Meals
  Noodly Chicken & Green Bean Skillet, 38
  Spanish Skillet Supper, 62
  Tex-Mex Beef & Black Bean Skillet, 122
Sloppy Joe Rollers, 149
Sloppy Onion Joes, 86
Sonoma Burgers Stuffed with Blue Cheese, 146
Southern-Style Chicken and Greens, 42
Southwest Chicken, 72
Southwestern Chicken Soup, 22
Southwestern Meat Loaf, 88
Spaghetti with Fresh Tomato Sauce, 200
Spanish Skillet Supper, 62
Special Occasion Meat Loaf, 85
Speedy Beef & Bean Burrito, 154
Spicy Fried Chicken, 44
Spicy Mango Chicken, 66
Spicy Quick and Easy Chili, 135
Spicy Wings, 10
Spinach
  Chicken Tortellini Soup, 171
  Crispy Lemon Pepper Chicken with Spinach Pasta, 210
  Greens and Gemelli, 208
  Joe's Special, 116
  Lasagna Beef 'n' Spinach Roll-Ups, 112
  Pesto & Tortellini Soup, 170
  Quick Greek Pitas, 121
  San Francisco Grilled Chicken, 80
  Special Occasion Meat Loaf, 85
  Spinach-Potato Bake, 100
Sticky Wings, 6
String Pie, 106
Stuffed Mexican Pizza Pie, 109
Sun-Dried Tomato Pesto, 230
Sunshine Chicken Drumsticks, 10

Sweet and Sour Beef, 152
Sweet & Spicy Drumettes, 17
Swiss 'n' Chicken Casserole, 46
Szechuan Cold Noodles, 222
Szechwan Beef, 121

T
Taco Chicken Nachos, 4
Taco Pot Pie, 124
Taco Salad, 186
Tacos in Pasta Shells, 102
Taco Taters, 150
Tamale Pie, 110
Tempting Taco Burgers, 90
Teriyaki Burgers, 158
Texas Beef Stew, 132
Texas-Style Chili, 140
Tex-Mex Beef & Black Bean Skillet, 122
30-Minute Chili Mac, 202
Tomato and Turkey Soup with Pesto,
      162
Tomato Chicken Gumbo, 24
Tomato-Eggplant Sauce, 234
Tomatoes, Fresh
   Albóndigas Soup, 128
   Basil Shrimp Fettuccine, 204
   BLT Chicken Salad for Two, 26
   California Chef Salad, 32
   Chicken Shish-Kebabs, 74
   Cobb Salad with Tarragon Dressing,
      26
   Deep Dish All-American Pizza, 84
   Fresh 'n' Sassy Spaghetti Sauce, 228
   Garden Pasta Salad, 180
   Grilled Chicken and Vegetable
      Kabobs, 78
   Italian Vegetable Salad, 190
   Main-Dish Pie, 160
   Malaysian Curried Beef, 100
   Mango & Black Bean Salsa, 66
   Mediterranean Burgers, 88
   Pasta Beef & Zucchini Dinner, 120
   Pasta Pesto Salad, 178
   Pasta "Pizza," 101
   Pepperoni Pasta Salad, 178, 216
   Peppery Grilled Salad, 71
   Pesto Chicken Brushetta, 12
   Quick Greek Pitas, 121
   Roasted Fresh Tomatoes, 191
   Salsa Sauce, 234
   Saucy Stuffed Peppers, 90
   Southwestern Chicken Soup, 22
   Spaghetti with Fresh Tomato Sauce, 200
   Taco Chicken Nachos, 4

Tomatoes, Fresh (continued)
   Taco Pot Pie, 124
   Taco Salad, 186
   Tempting Taco Burgers, 90
   Tuscany Chicken Soup, 164
Tortellini Vegetable Soup, 162
Tortilla Crunch Chicken Fingers, 17
Tropical Chicken Salad, 28
Tropical Salad Dressing, 28
Tuna Mac, 196
Turkey
   California Chef Salad, 32
   Minute Minestrone Soup, 174
   Tomato and Turkey Soup with Pesto,
      162
   Tortellini Vegetable Soup, 162
Tuscan Chicken and Pasta, 194
Tuscany Chicken Soup, 164

U
Ultimate Macaroni & Cheese, 212

V
Vegetable Almond Fettuccine, 208

W
Walnut Lemon Couscous, 220
Western Hash, 157
Western Wagon Wheels, 124
White Cheddar Seafood Chowder, 171
Wild Mushroom Sauce, 230
Wild Rice Soup, 141

Z
Zesty Pasta Salad, 192
Zucchini
   Antipasto Salad, 192
   Beef & Zucchini Quiche, 109
   Chicken Rotini Soup, 172
   Couscous with Vegetables in Savory
      Broth, 224
   Farmer's Stew Argentina, 140
   Garden Pasta Salad, 180
   Greek Beef & Rice, 118
   Grilled Chicken and Vegetable
      Kabobs, 78
   Grilled Vegetable and Chicken Pasta, 78
   Italian Vegetable Salad, 190
   Pasta Beef & Zucchini Dinner, 120
   Pasta Primavera, 214
   Sicilian-Style Pasta Salad, 184
   Southwestern Chicken Soup, 22
   Tuscan Chicken and Pasta, 194
   Zucchini Lasagne, 101